Ninja Foodi 2-Basket Air Fryer Cookbook

Effortless, Delicious & Easy Recipes for Smart People on a Budget
(Air Fry, Air Broil, Roast, Bake, Reheat, and Dehydrate)

Dorela Jeran

© Copyright 2020 Dorela Jeran - All Rights Reserved.

In no way is it legal to reproduce, duplicate, or transmit any part of this document by either electronic means or in printed format. Recording of this publication is strictly prohibited, and any storage of this material is not allowed unless with written permission from the publisher. All rights reserved.

The information provided herein is stated to be truthful and consistent, in that any liability, regarding inattention or otherwise, by any usage or abuse of any policies, processes, or directions contained within is the solitary and complete responsibility of the recipient reader. Under no circumstances will any legal liability or blame be held against the publisher for any reparation, damages, or monetary loss due to the information herein, either directly or indirectly.

Respective authors own all copyrights not held by the publisher.

Legal Notice:

This book is copyright protected. This is only for personal use. You cannot amend, distribute, sell, use, quote or paraphrase any part of the content within this book without the consent of the author or copyright owner. Legal action will be pursued if this is breached.

Disclaimer Notice:

Please note the information contained within this document is for educational and entertainment purposes only. Every attempt has been made to provide accurate, up-to-date and reliable, complete information. No warranties of any kind are expressed or implied. Readers acknowledge that the author is not engaging in the rendering of legal, financial, medical or professional advice.

By reading this document, the reader agrees that under no circumstances are we responsible for any losses, direct or indirect, which are incurred as a result of the use of information contained within this document, including, but not limited to, errors, omissions, or inaccuracies.

Table of Contents

Chapter 1: Understanding the Ninja Foodi Dual Zone Air Fryer 6
    The Benefits of Using Ninja Foodi Dual Zone Air Fryer 6
    Structural Composition of the Ninja Foodi Dual Zone Air Fryer 7

Chapter 2: How to Use the Ninja Foodi 2 Basket Air Fryer 10

Chapter 3: Breakfast Recipes 12
    Turkey Morning Patties 12
    Potato Hash Browns 13
    Air Fried Breakfast Sausage 14
    Egg Pepper Cups 15
    Crispy Breakfast Bacon 16
    Egg Bacon Balls 17
    Crispy Egg Rolls 19
    Spinach Egg Cups 21
    Pumpkin Muffins 22
    French Toast Sticks 23

Chapter 4: Snacks and Appetizers 24
    Chicken Wraps 24
    Chicken Mushroom Bites 25
    Onion Rings 26
    Potato Tater Tots 28
    Plantain Chips 29
    Crispy Asparagus 30
    Breaded Ravioli 31
    Tortilla Chips 32

Chapter 5: Beef, Lamb and Pork 33
    Pork with Potatoes and Green Beans 33
    Mini Meatloaves 35
    Pork Chops with Brussels Sprouts 36
    Italian Meatballs 37
    Pork Chops with Broccoli Florets 39
    Parmesan Pork Chops 40
    Beef Cheeseburgers 41
    Lamb Shank with Mushroom Stir Fry 42
    Korean Brisket 43

Beef Bites with Chipotle Dip	44
Vegetable Pork Skewers	45
Dijon Lamb Chops	46
Beef-Pepper Kabobs	47
Sriracha Steak Skewers	48
Pork Pineapple Skewers	49
Pork Skewers with Mango Salsa	50
Chapter 6: Poultry	**52**
Chicken Katsu	52
Bacon-Wrapped Chicken Thighs	54
Bang-Bang Chicken	56
Tso's Chicken	57
Chicken Wing Drumettes	59
Crusted Chicken Breast	60
Crispy Chicken Fillets	61
Chicken Potatoes Mix	63
Air Fried Turkey Breast	64
Chili Chicken Wings	65
Turkey Mushroom Burgers	67
Brazilian Chicken	68
Chapter 7: Seafood and Fish	**69**
Spinach Scallops	69
Fish Finger Sandwich	70
Lobster Tails	71
Buttered Mahi Mahi	72
Salmon Fillets with Fennel Salad	73
Sweet Salmon Fillets	74
Crusted Cod Fish	75
Glazed Scallops	76
Crusted Tilapia Fillets	77
Crispy Catfish Fillets	78
Shrimp Scampi	79
Salmon Nuggets	80
Chapter 8: Vegetables	**81**
Easy Air Fried Tofu	81
Chickpea Falafel	82

Gingered Carrots	84
Zucchini Fritters	85
Quinoa Burger	86
Air Fried Okra	88
Hasselback Potatoes	89
Chapter 9: Desserts	**90**
Mini Apple Pies	90
Walnuts Fritters	92
Air Fried Bananas	94
Crispy Beignets	95
Cinnamon Doughnuts	96
Cranberry Scones	97
Apple Flautas	98
Apple Oats Crisp	100
Conclusion	**101**

Chapter 1: Understanding the Ninja Foodi Dual Zone Air Fryer

Do you want to cut your cooking time to half? Or do you want to cook two meals at a time? Then the new Ninja Foodi Dual Zone Air fryer is the next good thing that you should buy for your kitchen. This Air fryer is designed with a dual-zone technology that will let you cook two different meals at a time either on a single cooking mode and setting or two different modes and settings. While this might sound too good to be true but Ninja Kitchen has made it possible. In a single 8 quart Ninja Air fryer, your cooking options will be multiplied up to many folds because this time, you will be having two air fryer basket and two independent cooking zones. Handling two fryer baskets at a time may sound too complicated, but Ninja kitchen has managed to create such a simple and user-friendly control system with a touch button panel that will let you choose and select any program, any cooking temperature, and time for both the cooking chambers independently or in complete sync with another. Doesn't that sound amazing? Well, it does! And if you are up for more surprises, then continue reading as we are about to discuss some major benefits of this Dual Zone Air fryer.

The Benefits of Using Ninja Foodi Dual Zone Air Fryer

The Ninja 2 basket Air Fry is known for several of its advanced features and its ultimate benefits.

1. Smart Finish

This cooking miracle can intelligently sync the cook times of both the cooking zones so that you cook different foods at a time with the same finishing time. So, here is how it works! When you add different food to the two baskets, and each has its own cooking time. When you cook using the smart cooking function and start the operation, the basket with the longer cooking time will initiate its operation first while the other basket will stay on hold until the other chamber reaches the same cooking time. In this way, both sides finish cooking at the same time.

2. Match Cook

The total 8 quartz capacity of this Ninja Air fryer is divided into two 4 quarts air fryer baskets, which means that you get to cook different food and the same food in the two baskets at a time. Using the match cook technology, you can use the same cooking function for both the baskets and use its XL capacity.

3. XL 8-Qt. Capacity

The large 8 quarts capacity divide into two parts gives you a perfect space to cook food in a large and small amount. This capacity is enough to cook 2 lbs of fries and 2 lbs of wings and drumettes.

4. Nonstick For Easy Cleaning

Both two baskets are nonstick, so they are easy to clean and wash. Crisper plates that are lined at the base of the baskets are dishwasher safe so you can wash them without damaging them.

Structural Composition of the Ninja Foodi Dual Zone Air Fryer

The Digital Ninja Foodi Air Fry has brought such a revolution into the kitchen that now the users can enjoy fresh and crispy meals in no time. It is a dual-zone air fryer technology that has merged 6 cooking functions like the Air Broil, Air Fry, Roast, Bake, Dehydrate and Reheat. This appliance is especially good for people who love to bake and cook crispy food.

The air fryer comes with 2 Fryer baskets that are marked as "1" and "2," and each should be inserted into their respective portions because of their different shapes. The baskets don't have any click button to open. You can simply remove them by pulling them out.

The control panel is present right on top of the Basket's inlets, and it covers the front top portion of the Air fryer. The top of the air fryer unit is flat, and it does not produce much heat. Do not place anything on the flat top of the air fryer unit or nearby. The control panel is designed with function and operating buttons.

The display screen is divided into two sections, each indicating the cooking status of its side of the basket. To select the settings for basket 1, press the KEY 1 on the control panel, and to select the settings for basket 2, press the KEY2 on the control. The other function and operating keys include:

Function Buttons:

- AIR BROIL: This mode gives a crispy touch to the meals and uses it to melt the toppings of the food

- AIR FRY: Cook crispy fried food without the use of the oil with the help of this mode.
- ROAST: Turn this air fryer unit into a roaster oven to cook soft and tender meat.
- BAKE: Cooked delicious baked desserts and treats.
- REHEAT: Allow you to reheat and warm your leftovers meals.
- DEHYDRATE: Use this mode to dehydrate fruits, meats, and vegetables.

Operating Buttons:

- TEMP Keys: The up and down key allows you to adjust the cooking temperature.
- TIME arrows: The up and down keys are there to adjust the cooking time.
- SMART FINISH button: This mode automatically syncs the cooking times of both the cooking zones and let them finish at the same time.
- MATCH COOK button: Allow you to automatically match the settings of zone 2 to those of the first cooking zone, which lets you cook a larger amount of the same food or different type of food in the same settings.
- START/PAUSE button: These buttons are used to initiate, stop, and resume the cooking.
- POWER BUTTON: The button is pressed to turn on or off the unit once the cooking function is completed or stopped.
- Standby Mode: In this mode, the Power button will get dimly lit, and the machine goes into standby if there is no activity for 10 minutes.
- Hold Mode: Hold sign will appear on the display screen when it is in the SMART FINISH mode. When the cooking time of one zone is greater than the other, then the hold will appear for the zone with less cooking time until its cooking time matches with the other one.

The Dual-Zone Technology

The amazing dual-zone technology of the Ninja Air fryer will let you cook using the following two modes:

- Smart Finish Technology

This function is used to finish cooking at the same time when foods in the two air fryer baskets have different cook temps, times, or even cooking functions:

1. Add all the ingredients into the baskets, then insert baskets in the air fryer unit.

2. Press the smart finish mode, and the machine will automatically sync during cooking.
3. At first, the Zone 1 will stay illuminated. Now select the cooking function for this zone. Use the TEMP key to set the required temperature, and use the TIME keys to set the required time.
4. Now select zone 2, and select the cooking function.
5. Use the TEMP keys to set the temperature, then use the TIME key to set the time for zone 2.
6. Press the start button, and the timer will start ticking for both zones according to their timings. And the cooking will be finished at one time.
7. On smart finish mode, you can also start cooking at the same time and let it end at different times. For that, simply select their cooking time and press the start button for both zones.

- Match Cook

To cook a larger amount of the same food, or cook different foods using the same function, temperature, and time:

1. Add the cooking ingredients into the baskets, then insert both the baskets into the unit.
2. Zone 1 will stay illuminated. Press the desired function button. Use the TEMP keys to set the cooking temperature, and use the TIME keys to set the time.
3. Press the MATCH COOK button to copy the basket one's settings to the basket 2.
4. Then press the START/PAUSE button to initiate cooking in both the baskets.
5. Once the cooking is completed "End" sign will appear on both the screens.

Chapter 2: How to Use the Ninja Foodi 2 Basket Air Fryer

To use the different cooking programs of the Ninja Foodi Air Fryer, you can try the following steps:

Air Broil:

1. Insert crisper plate in the basket, then add ingredients into the basket, and insert basket in the unit.
2. The unit will default to zone 1, and to use zone 2 instead, select zone 2.
3. Select the Air broil cooking mode.
4. Use the TEMP keys to set the desired temperature.
5. Use the TIME key to set the time from 1-minute to 1 hour and from 5-minute to 1 to 4 hours.
6. Press the START/PAUSE button to initiate cooking.
7. The unit will beep once the cooking is complete, and the "End" sign will appear on the display screen.
8. Remove ingredients from the basket/s by dumping them out onto the plate or using silicone tongs/utensils.

Air Fry:

1. Insert crisper plate in the basket, then add ingredients into the basket, and insert basket in the unit.
2. The unit will default to zone 1, and to use basket 2 instead of just select zone 2.
3. Select Air Fry cooking mode use the TEMP keys to set the required temperature.
4. Use the TIME keys to set the time from 1-minute to 1 hour and from 5-minute from 1 to 4 hours.
5. Press the START/PAUSE button to initiate cooking.
6. The unit will beep once the cooking is completed, and the "End" sign will appear on display.

Bake:

1. Insert crisper plate in the basket, then add ingredients into the basket, and insert basket in the unit.
2. Select BAKE cooking mode. Use the TEMP keys to set the required temperature.
3. Use the TIME keys to set the time in 1-minute increments up to 1 hour and in 5-minute increments from 1 to 4 hours.

4. Press the START/PAUSE button to begin cooking.
5. The unit will beep once the cooking is complete, and the "End" sign will appear on the display screen.
6. Reduce the temperature by 25 degrees F while converting the traditional oven recipes.

Other Cooking Modes:

While using the other cooking modes, remember to follow the same steps, and select use the crisper plate or cooking rack as required. Then select the required mode, zone, and temperature then initiate cooking.

You can remove any of the baskets during the cooking process and shake the food inside, then reinsert the baskets to resume cooking. Press the start button to resume cooking.

The broiling function is not available for the MATCH COOK technology; you can only broil the food in one basket at a time. If your food is in a large amount and you need to broil it, then broil in batches.

Cleaning and Maintenance:

Here is how you can keep your 2 basket air fryer clean and maintained after every session of cooking:

1. Unplug the appliance before cleaning it and allow it to cool completely.
2. You can remove the air fryer baskets from the main unit and keep them aside to cool.
3. Once cooled, remove their air crisper plates and wash them in the dishwasher.
4. Clean the air fryer basket using soapy water and avoid hard scrubbing to protect their nonstick layers.
5. Dishwash the air fryer racks in the dishwasher and use soft scrubs if the food is stuck to the rack.
6. Wipe the main unit with a clean piece of cloth or with a lightly damp cloth.
7. Once everything is cleaned and return the baskets to the air fryer.
8. Now your device is ready to use.

Chapter 3: Breakfast Recipes

Turkey Morning Patties

Prep Time: 10 minutes
Cooking Time: 13 minutes
Serving: 8

Ingredients

- 2 tsp fennel seeds
- 1 lb pork mince
- 2 tsp dry rubbed sage
- 1 lb turkey mince
- 2 tsp garlic powder
- 1 tsp paprika
- 1 tsp sea salt
- 1 tsp dried thyme

Method:

1. In a mixing bowl, add turkey and pork then mix them together.
2. Mix sage, fennel, paprika, salt, thyme, and garlic powder in a small bowl.
3. Drizzle this mixture over the meat mixture and mix well.
4. Take 2 tbsp of this mixture at a time and roll it into thick patties.
5. Place half of the patties in the Basket 1, and the other half in basket 2 then spray them all with cooking oil.
6. Return the Air Fryer Baskets to the Air Fryer.
7. Select the Air Fryer mode for Zone 1 with 390 degrees F temperature and 13 minutes cooking time.
8. Press the MATCH COOK button to copy the settings for Zone 2.
9. Initiate cooking by pressing the START/PAUSE BUTTON.
10. Flip the patties in the baskets once cooked halfway through.
11. Serve warm and fresh.

Nutritional Information per Serving:

- Calories 184
- Total Fat 7.9 g
- Saturated Fat 1.4 g
- Cholesterol 36 mg
- Sodium 704 mg
- Total Carbs 6 g
- Fiber 3.6 g
- Sugar 5.5 g
- Protein 17.9 g

Potato Hash Browns

Prep Time: 10 minutes
Cooking Time: 13 minutes
Serving: 6

Ingredients

- 3 russet potatoes
- ¼ cup chopped green peppers
- ¼ cup chopped red peppers
- ¼ cup chopped onions
- 2 garlic cloves chopped
- 1 tsp paprika
- Salt and black pepper, to taste
- 2 tsp olive oil

Method:

1. Peel and grate all the potatoes with the help of a cheese grater.
2. Add potato shreds to a bowl filled with cold water and leave it soaked for 25 minutes.
3. Drain the water and place the potato shreds in a plate lined with a paper towel.
4. Transfer the shreds to a dry bowl and add olive oil, paprika, garlic, and black pepper.
5. Make four flat patties out of the potato mixture and place two into each of the Air fryer baskets.
6. Return the Air Fryer Baskets to the Air Fryer.
7. Select the Air Fryer mode for Zone 1 with 390 degrees F temperature and 13 minutes cooking time.
8. Press the MATCH COOK button to copy the settings for Zone 2.
9. Initiate cooking by pressing the START/PAUSE BUTTON.
10. Flip the potato hash browns once cooked halfway through, then resume cooking.
11. Once done, serve warm.

Nutritional Information per Serving:

- Calories 134
- Total Fat 4.7 g
- Saturated Fat 0.6 g
- Cholesterol 124mg
- Sodium 1 mg
- Total Carbs 54.1 g
- Fiber 7 g
- Sugar 3.3 g
- Protein 6.2 g

Air Fried Breakfast Sausage

Prep Time: 10 minutes
Cooking Time: 13 minutes
Serving: 4

Ingredients

- 4 sausage links, raw and uncooked

Method:

1. Divide the sausages in the two Air fryer baskets.
2. Return the Air Fryer Baskets to the Air Fryer.
3. Select the Air Fryer mode for Zone 1 with 390 degrees F temperature and 13 minutes cooking time.
4. Press the MATCH COOK button to copy the settings for Zone 2.
5. Initiate cooking by pressing the START/PAUSE BUTTON.
6. Serve warm and fresh.

Nutritional Information per Serving:

- Calories 187
- Total Fat 6 g
- Saturated Fat 9.9 g
- Cholesterol 41 mg
- Sodium 154 mg
- Total Carbs 7.4 g
- Fiber 2.9 g
- Sugar 15.3 g
- Protein 24.6 g

Egg Pepper Cups

Prep Time: 10 minutes
Cooking Time: 12 minutes
Serving: 4

Ingredients

- 2 bell pepper, halved, seeds removed
- 8 eggs
- 1 tsp olive oil
- 1 pinch salt and black pepper
- 1 pinch sriracha flakes

Method:

1. Slice the bell peppers in half, lengthwise and remove their seeds and the inner portion to get cup-like shape.
2. Rub olive oil on the edges of the bell peppers.
3. Place them in the two Air Fryer Baskets with their cut side up and crack two eggs in each half of bell pepper.
4. Drizzle salt, black pepper, and sriracha flakes on top of the eggs.
5. Return the Air Fryer Baskets to the Air Fryer.
6. Select the Air Fryer mode for Zone 1 with 390 degrees F temperature and 18 minutes cooking time.
7. Press the MATCH COOK button to copy the settings for Zone 2.
8. Initiate cooking by pressing the START/PAUSE BUTTON.
9. Serve warm and fresh.

Nutritional Information per Serving:

- Calories 212
- Total Fat 11.8 g
- Saturated Fat 2.2 g
- Cholesterol 23mg
- Sodium 321 mg
- Total Carbs 14.6 g
- Dietary Fiber 4.4 g
- Sugar 8 g
- Protein 17.3 g

Crispy Breakfast Bacon

Prep Time: 10 minutes
Cooking Time: 14 minutes
Serving: 6

Ingredients

- ½ lb of bacon slices

Method:

1. Spread half of the bacon slices in each of the Air Fryer baskets evenly in a single layer.
2. Return the Air Fryer Baskets to the Air Fryer.
3. Select the Air Fryer mode for Zone 1 with 390 degrees F temperature and 14 minutes cooking time.
4. Press the MATCH COOK button to copy the settings for Zone 2.
5. Initiate cooking by pressing the START/PAUSE BUTTON.
6. Flip the crispy bacon once cooked halfway through, then resume cooking.
7. Serve.

Nutritional Information per Serving:

- Calories 142
- Total Fat 24.8 g
- Saturated Fat 12.4 g
- Cholesterol 3 mg
- Sodium 132 mg
- Total Carbs 0.8 g
- Dietary Fiber 3.9 g
- Sugar 2.5 g
- Protein 18.9 g

Egg Bacon Balls

Prep Time: 10 minutes
Cooking Time: 14 minutes
Serving: 6

Ingredients

- 1 tbsp butter
- 2 eggs, beaten
- ¼ tsp pepper
- 1 can (10.2 oz) Pillsbury Buttermilk biscuits
- 2 oz cheddar cheese, diced into ten cubes
- Cooking spray
- Egg Wash
- 1 egg
- 1 tbsp water

Method:

1. Place a suitable non-stick skillet over medium-high heat and cook the bacon until crispy, then place it in a plate lined with a paper towel.
2. Melt butter in the same skillet over medium heat. Beat eggs with pepper in a bowl and pour them in the skillet.
3. Stir cook for 5 minutes then remove it from the heat.
4. Add bacon and mix well.
5. Divide the dough into 5 biscuits and slice each into 2 layers.
6. Press each biscuit into 4 inches round.
7. Add a tbsp of egg mixture at the center of each round and top it with a piece of cheese.
8. Carefully fold the biscuit dough around the filling and pinch the edges to seal.
9. Whisk egg with water in a small bowl and brush the egg wash over the biscuits.
10. Place the half of the biscuit bombs in each of the Air Fryer Baskets and spray them with cooking oil.
11. Return the Air Fryer Baskets to the Air Fryer.
12. Select the Air Fryer mode for Zone 1 with 375 degrees F temperature and 14 minutes cooking time.
13. Press the MATCH COOK button to copy the settings for Zone 2.
14. Initiate cooking by pressing the START/PAUSE BUTTON.
15. Flip the egg bombs when cooked halfway through, then resume cooking.
16. Serve warm.

Nutritional Information per Serving:

- Calories 331
- Total Fat 2.5 g
- Saturated Fat 0.5 g
- Cholesterol 35 mg
- Sodium 595 mg
- Total Carbs 29 g
- Fiber 12.2 g
- Sugar 12.5 g
- Protein 18.7g

Crispy Egg Rolls

Prep Time: 10 minutes
Cooking Time: 13 minutes
Serving: 6

Ingredients

- 2 eggs
- 2 tbsp milk
- Salt, to taste
- Black pepper, to taste
- 1/2 cup shredded cheddar cheese
- 2 sausage patties
- 6 egg roll wrappers
- 1 tbsp olive oil
- 1 cup of water

Method:

1. Grease a small skillet with some olive oil and place it over medium heat.
2. Add sausage patties and cook them until brown.
3. Chop the cooked patties into small pieces. Beat eggs with salt, black pepper, and milk in a mixing bowl.
4. Grease the same skillet with 1 tsp olive oil and pour the egg mixture into it.
5. Stir cook to make scrambled eggs.
6. Add sausage, mix well and remove the skillet from the heat.
7. Spread an egg roll wrapper on the working surface in a diamond shape position.
8. Add a tbsp of cheese at the bottom third of the roll wrapper.
9. Top the cheese with egg mixture and wet the edges of the wrapper with water.
10. Fold the two corners of the wrapper and roll it then seal the edges.
11. Repeat the same steps and divide the rolls in the two Air Fryer Baskets.
12. Return the Air Fryer Baskets to the Air Fryer.
13. Select the Air Fryer mode for Zone 1 with 375 degrees F temperature and 13 minutes cooking time.
14. Press the MATCH COOK button to copy the settings for Zone 2.
15. Initiate cooking by pressing the START/PAUSE BUTTON.
16. Flip the rolls after 8 minutes and continue cooking for another 5 mintues.
17. Serve warm and fresh.

Nutritional Information per Serving:

- Calories 322
- Total Fat 11.8 g

- Saturated Fat 2.2 g
- Cholesterol 56 mg
- Sodium 321 mg
- Total Carbs 14.6 g
- Dietary Fiber 4.4 g
- Sugar 8 g
- Protein 17.3 g

Spinach Egg Cups

Prep Time: 10 minutes
Cooking Time: 13 minutes
Serving: 4

Ingredients

- 4 tbsp milk
- 4 tbsp frozen spinach, thawed
- 4 large egg
- 8 tsp grated cheese
- Salt, to taste
- Black pepper, to taste
- Cooking Spray

Method:

1. Grease four small sized ramekin with cooking spray.
2. Add egg, cheese, spinach, and milk to a bowl and beat well.
3. Divide the mixture into the four small ramekins and top them with salt and black pepper.
4. Place the two ramekins in each of the two Air Fryer Baskets.
5. Return the Air Fryer Baskets to the Air Fryer.
6. Select the Air Fryer mode for Zone 1 with 390 degrees F temperature and 13 minutes cooking time.
7. Press the MATCH COOK button to copy the settings for Zone 2.
8. Initiate cooking by pressing the START/PAUSE BUTTON.
9. Serve warm.

Nutritional Information per Serving:

- Calories 197
- Total Fat 15.4 g
- Saturated Fat 4.2 g
- Cholesterol 168 mg
- Sodium 203 mg
- Total Carbs 8.5 g
- Sugar 1.1 g
- Fiber 4 g
- Protein 17.9 g

Pumpkin Muffins

Prep Time: 10 minutes
Cooking Time: 13 minutes
Serving: 6

Ingredients

- ½ cup pumpkin puree
- 1 cup gluten-free oats
- ¼ cup honey
- 1 medium egg beaten
- ½ tsp coconut butter
- ½ tbsp cocoa nib
- ½ tbsp vanilla essence
- Cooking spray
- ½ tsp nutmeg

Method:

1. Add oats, honey, eggs, pumpkin puree, coconut butter, cocoa nibs, vanilla essence, and nutmeg to a bowl and mix well until smooth.
2. Divide the batter in two 4-cups muffin trays, greased with cooking spray.
3. Place one mini muffin tray in each of the two Air Fryer Baskets.
4. Return the Air Fryer Baskets to the Air Fryer.
5. Select the Air Fryer mode for Zone 1 with 375 degrees F temperature and 13 minutes cooking time.
6. Press the MATCH COOK button to copy the settings for Zone 2.
7. Initiate cooking by pressing the START/PAUSE BUTTON.
8. Allow the muffins to cool then serve.

Nutritional Information per Serving:

- Calories 138
- Total Fat 9.7 g
- Saturated Fat 4.7 g
- Cholesterol 181 mg
- Sodium 245 mg
- Total Carbs 32.5 g
- Fiber 0.3 g
- Sugar 1.8 g
- Protein 10.3 g

French Toast Sticks

Prep Time: 10 minutes
Cooking Time: 8 minutes
Serving: 2

Ingredients

- 4 pieces of bread
- 2 tbsp butter
- 2 eggs, beaten
- 1 pinch salt
- 1 pinch cinnamon ground
- 1 pinch nutmeg ground
- 1 pinch ground clove
- 1 tsp icing sugar

Method:

1. Add two eggs to a mixing bowl and stir cinnamon, nutmeg, ground cloves, and salt, then whisk well.
2. Spread butter on both sides of the bread slices and cut them into thick strips.
3. Dip the breadsticks in the egg mixture and place them in the two Air Fryer baskets.
4. Return the Air Fryer Baskets to the Air Fryer.
5. Select the Air Fryer mode for Zone 1 with 390 degrees F temperature and 8 minutes cooking time.
6. Press the MATCH COOK button to copy the settings for Zone 2.
7. Initiate cooking by pressing the START/PAUSE BUTTON.
8. Flip the french toast sticks when cooked halfway through.
9. Serve.

Nutritional Information per Serving:

- Calories 391
- Total Fat 2.8 g
- Saturated Fat 0.6 g
- Cholesterol 330 mg
- Sodium 62 mg
- Total Carbs 36.5 g
- Fiber 9.2 g
- Sugar 4.5 g
- Protein 6.6

Chapter 4: Snacks and Appetizers

Chicken Wraps

Prep Time: 10 minutes
Cooking Time: 12 minutes
Serving: 4

Ingredients

- 2 skinless, boneless cooked chicken breasts, cubed
- 3 tbsp chopped onion
- 3 garlic cloves, peeled and minced
- 3/4 (8 oz.) package cream cheese
- 6 tbsp butter
- 3 (10 oz.) cans refrigerated crescent roll dough

Method:

1. Heat oil in a skillet and add onion and garlic to sauté until soft.
2. Add cooked chicken, sautéed veggies, butter, and cream cheese to a blender.
3. Blend well until smooth. Spread the crescent dough over a flat surface.
4. Slice the dough into 12 rectangles.
5. Spoon the chicken mixture at the center of each rectangle.
6. Roll the dough to wrap the mixture and form a ball.
7. Divide these balls in the two Air Fryer baskets.
8. Return the Air Fryer Baskets to the Air Fryer.
9. Select the Air Fryer mode for Zone 1 with 390 degrees F temperature and 12 minutes cooking time.
10. Press the MATCH COOK button to copy the settings for Zone 2.
11. Initiate cooking by pressing the START/PAUSE BUTTON.
12. Serve warm.

Nutritional Information per Serving:

- Calories 153
- Total Fat 2.4 g
- Saturated Fat 3 g
- Cholesterol 21 mg
- Sodium 216 mg
- Total Carbs 18 g
- Fiber 2.3 g
- Sugar 1.2 g
- Protein 23.2 g

Chicken Mushroom Bites

Prep Time: 10 minutes
Cooking Time: 15 minutes
Serving: 6

Ingredients

- 6 large fresh mushrooms, stems removed

Stuffing:

- ½ cup chicken meat, cubed
- 1 (4 oz.) package cream cheese, softened
- ¼ lb. imitation crabmeat, flaked
- 1 cup butter
- 1 garlic clove, peeled and minced
- Black pepper and salt to taste
- Garlic powder to taste
- Crushed red pepper to taste

Method:

1. Melt and heat butter in a skillet over medium heat.
2. Add chicken and sauté for 5 minutes.
3. Add in all the remaining ingredients for the stuffing.
4. Cook for 5 minutes then turn off the heat.
5. Allow the mixture to cool. Stuff each mushroom with a tbsp of this mixture.
6. Divide the stuffed mushrooms in the two Air Fryer baskets.
7. Return the Air Fryer Baskets to the Air Fryer.
8. Select the Air Fryer mode for Zone 1 with 375 degrees F temperature and 15 minutes cooking time.
9. Press the MATCH COOK button to copy the settings for Zone 2.
10. Initiate cooking by pressing the START/PAUSE BUTTON.
11. Serve warm.

Nutritional Information per Serving:

- Calories 129
- Total Fat 17 g
- Saturated Fat 3 g
- Cholesterol 65 mg
- Sodium 391 mg
- Total Carbs 55 g
- Fiber 6 g
- Sugar 8 g
- Protein 14g

Onion Rings

Prep Time: 10 minutes
Cooking Time: 22 minutes
Serving: 4

Ingredients

- ¾ cup all-purpose flour
- 1 tsp salt
- 1 large onion, cut into rings
- ½ cup cornstarch
- 2 tsp baking powder
- 1 cup low-fat milk
- 1 egg
- 1 cup bread crumbs
- 1/6 tsp paprika
- Cooking spray
- 1/6 tsp garlic powder

Method:

1. Mix flour with baking powder, cornstarch, and salt in a small bowl.
2. First coat the onion rings with flour mixture; set them aside.
3. Beat milk with egg then add remaining flour mixture into the egg.
4. Mix them well together to make a thick batter.
5. Now dip the floured onion rings into the prepared batter and coat them well.
6. Place the rings on a wire rack for 10 minutes.
7. Spread bread crumbs in a shallow bowl.
8. Coat the onion rings with breadcrumbs and shake off the excess.
9. Set the coated onion rings in the two Air fryer baskets.
10. Spray all the rings with the cooking spray.
11. Return the Air Fryer Baskets to the Air Fryer.
12. Select the Air Fryer mode for Zone 1 with 375 degrees F temperature and 22 minutes cooking time.
13. Press the MATCH COOK button to copy the settings for Zone 2.
14. Initiate cooking by pressing the START/PAUSE BUTTON.
15. Flip once cooked halfway through, then resume cooking
16. Season the air fried onion rings with garlic powder and paprika.
17. Serve.

Nutritional Information per Serving:

- Calories 297
- Total Fat 14 g

- Saturated Fat 5 g
- Cholesterol 99 mg
- Sodium 364 mg
- Total Carbs 28 g
- Fiber 1 g
- Sugar 3 g
- Protein 3 g

Potato Tater Tots

Prep Time: 10 minutes
Cooking Time: 27 minutes
Serving: 4

Ingredients

- 2 potatoes, peeled
- 1/2 tsp Cajun seasoning
- Olive oil cooking spray
- Sea salt to taste

Method:

1. Boil water in a cooking pot and cook potatoes in it for 15 minutes.
2. Drain and leave the potatoes to cool in a bowl.
3. Grate these potatoes and toss it with Cajun seasoning.
4. Make small tater tots out of this mixture.
5. Divide them in the two Air Fryer baskets and spray them with cooking oil.
6. Return the Air Fryer Baskets to the Air Fryer.
7. Select the Air Fryer mode for Zone 1 with 375 degrees F temperature and 27 minutes cooking time.
8. Press the MATCH COOK button to copy the settings for Zone 2.
9. Initiate cooking by pressing the START/PAUSE BUTTON.
10. Flip them once cooked halfway through, and resume cooking.
11. Serve warm.

Nutritional Information per Serving:

- Calories 152
- Total Fat 14 g
- Saturated Fat 2 g
- Cholesterol 65 mg
- Sodium 220 mg
- Total Carbs 35.8 g
- Fiber 0.2 g
- Sugar 1 g
- Protein 6 g

Plantain Chips

Prep Time: 10 minutes
Cooking Time: 20 minutes
Serving: 2

Ingredients

- 1 green plantain
- 1 tsp canola oil
- 1/2 tsp sea salt

Method:

1. Peel and cut the plantains into long strips using a mandolin slicer.
2. Grease the Air Fryer basket with a ½ tsp with canola oil.
3. Toss the plantains with salt and remaining canola oil.
4. Divide these plantains in the two Air fryer baskets.
5. Return the Air Fryer Baskets to the Air Fryer.
6. Select the Air Fryer mode for Zone 1 with 350 degrees F temperature and 20 minutes cooking time.
7. Press the MATCH COOK button to copy the settings for Zone 2.
8. Initiate cooking by pressing the START/PAUSE BUTTON.
9. Toss the plantains after 10 minutes and resume cooking.
10. Serve warm.

Nutritional Information per Serving:

- Calories 218
- Total Fat 8 g
- Saturated Fat 1 g
- Cholesterol 153mg
- sodium 339 mg
- Total Carbs 8 g
- Fiber 1 g
- Sugar 2 g
- Protein 3 g

Crispy Asparagus

Prep Time: 10 minutes
Cooking Time: 16 minutes
Serving: 4

Ingredients

- 1 bunch of asparagus, trimmed
- Avocado or Olive Oil
- Himalayan salt, to taste
- Black pepper, to taste

Method:

1. Divide the asparagus in the two Air Fryer baskets.
2. Toss the asparagus with salt, black pepper, and oil.
3. Return the Air Fryer Baskets to the Air Fryer.
4. Select the Air Fryer mode for Zone 1 with 390 degrees F temperature and 16 minutes cooking time.
5. Press the MATCH COOK button to copy the settings for Zone 2.
6. Initiate cooking by pressing the START/PAUSE BUTTON.
7. Serve warm.

Nutritional Information per Serving:

- Calories 301
- Total Fat 15.8 g
- Saturated Fat 2.7 g
- Cholesterol 75 mg
- Sodium 189 mg
- Total Carbs 31.7 g
- Fiber 0.3 g
- Sugar 0.1 g
- Protein 8.2 g

Breaded Ravioli

Prep Time: 10 minutes
Cooking Time: 15 minutes
Serving: 4

Ingredients

- 1 package ravioli, frozen
- 1 cup bread crumbs
- 1/2 cup parmesan cheese
- 1 tbsp Italian seasoning
- 1 tbsp garlic powder
- 2 eggs, beaten
- Cooking spray

Method:

1. Toss breadcrumbs with cheese, garlic powder, and Italian seasoning in a bowl.
2. Beat 2 eggs in another bowl and keep them aside.
3. Grease the Air Fryer's basket with cooking spray.
4. Dip ravioli first in egg mixture then coat it in the breadcrumb's mixture.
5. Divide the coated ravioli in the two Air fryer baskets.
6. Return the Air Fryer Baskets to the Air Fryer.
7. Select the Air Fryer mode for Zone 1 with 390 degrees F temperature and 15 minutes cooking time.
8. Press the MATCH COOK button to copy the settings for Zone 2.
9. Initiate cooking by pressing the START/PAUSE BUTTON.
10. Flip the crispy ravioli once cooked halfway through, then resume cooking.
11. Serve warm.

Nutritional Information per Serving:

- Calories 231
- Total Fat 20.1 g
- Saturated Fat 2.4 g
- Cholesterol 110 mg
- Sodium 941 mg
- Total Carbs 30.1 g
- Fiber 0.9 g
- Sugar 1.4 g
- Protein 4.6 g

Tortilla Chips

Prep Time: 10 minutes
Cooking Time: 13 minutes
Serving: 4

Ingredients

- 4 (6-inch) corn tortillas
- 1 tbsp Avocado Oil
- Sea salt to taste
- Cooking spray

Method:

1. Spread the corn tortillas on the working surface.
2. Slice them into bite-sized triangles.
3. Toss them with salt and cooking oil.
4. Divide the triangles in the two Air fryer baskets in a single layer.
5. Return the Air Fryer Baskets to the Air Fryer.
6. Select the Air Fryer mode for Zone 1 with 390 degrees F temperature and 13 minutes cooking time.
7. Press the MATCH COOK button to copy the settings for Zone 2.
8. Initiate cooking by pressing the START/PAUSE BUTTON.
9. Toss the chips once cooked halfway through, then resume cooking.
10. Serve and enjoy.

Nutritional Information per Serving:

- Calories 440
- Total Fat 7.9 g
- Saturated Fat 1.8 g
- Cholesterol 5 mg
- Sodium 581 mg
- Total Carbs 21.8 g
- Sugar 7.1 g
- Fiber 2.6 g
- Protein 37.2 g

Chapter 5: Beef, Lamb and Pork

Pork with Potatoes and Green Beans

Prep Time: 10 minutes
Cooking Time: 15 minutes
Serving: 2

Ingredients

- ¼ cup Dijon mustard
- 2 tbsp brown sugar
- 1 tsp dried parsley flake
- ½ tsp dried thyme
- ¼ tsp salt
- ¼ tsp ground black pepper
- 1 ¼ lbs pork tenderloin
- ¾ lb small potatoes, halved
- 1 (12 oz) package green beans, trimmed
- 1 tbsp olive oil
- Salt and black pepper ground to taste

Method:

1. Preheat your Air Fryer Machine to 400 F.
2. Add mustard, parsley, brown sugar, salt, black pepper, and thyme in a large bowl then mix well.
3. Add tenderloin to the spice mixture and coat well.
4. Toss potatoes with olive oil, salt, black pepper and green beans in another bowl.
5. Place the prepared tenderloin in Zone 1 Basket.
6. Return this Air Fryer Basket to the Air Fryer.
7. Select the Air Fryer mode for Zone 1 with 390 degrees F temperature and 15 minutes cooking time.
8. Add potatoes and green beans to the second Basket
9. Select the Air Fryer mode for Zone 2 with 350 degrees F temperature and 10 minutes cooking time.
10. Press the SMART FINISH button to sync the settings with Zone 2.
11. Initiate cooking by pressing the START/PAUSE BUTTON.
12. Serve the tenderloin with Air Fried potatoes.

Nutritional Information per Serving:

- Calories 380
- Total Fat 20 g
- Saturated Fat 5 g
- Cholesterol 151 mg

- Sodium 686 mg
- Total Carbs 33 g
- Fiber 1 g
- Sugar 1.2 g
- Protein 21 g

Mini Meatloaves

Prep Time: 10 minutes
Cooking Time: 22 minutes
Serving: 4

Ingredients

- ⅓ cup milk
- 2 tbsp basil pesto
- 1 egg, beaten
- 1 clove garlic, minced
- ¼ tsp ground black pepper
- 1 lb ground beef
- ⅓ cup panko bread crumbs
- 8 pepperoni slices
- 2 oz small mozzarella balls
- ½ cup marinara sauce, warmed
- 1 tbsp chopped fresh basil, or to taste

Method:

1. Mix pesto, milk, egg, garlic, and black pepper in a medium-sized bowl.
2. Stir in ground beef and bread crumbs then mix.
3. Make the 4 small sized loaves with this mixture and top them with 2 pepperoni slices.
4. Press the slices into the meatloaves.
5. Place the meatloaves in the two Air Fryer Baskets.
6. Return the Air Fryer Baskets to the Air Fryer.
7. Select the Air Fryer mode for Zone 1 with 390 degrees F temperature and 22 minutes cooking time.
8. Press the MATCH COOK button to copy the settings for Zone 2.
9. Initiate cooking by pressing the START/PAUSE BUTTON.
10. Top them with marinara sauce and basil to serve.
11. Serve warm.

Nutritional Information per Serving:

- Calories 361
- Total Fat 16.3 g
- Saturated Fat 4.9 g
- Cholesterol 114 mg
- Sodium 515 mg
- Total Carbs 19.3 g
- Fiber 0.1 g
- Sugar 18.2 g
- Protein 33.3 g

Pork Chops with Brussels Sprouts

Prep Time: 10 minutes
Cooking Time: 15 minutes
Serving: 4

Ingredients

- 4 bone-in center-cut pork chop
- Cooking spray
- Salt, to taste
- Black pepper, to taste
- 2 tsp olive oil
- 2 tsp pure maple syrup
- 2 tsp Dijon mustard
- 6 oz Brussels sprouts, quartered

Method:

1. Rub pork chop with salt, ¼ tsp black pepper, and cooking spray.
2. Toss brussels sprouts with mustard, syrup, oil, ¼ tsp black pepper in a medium bowl.
3. Add pork chop to the Zone 1 basket of the Air fryer.
4. Return the Air Fryer Basket to the Air Fryer.
5. Select the Air Fryer mode for Zone 1 with 400 degrees F temperature and 15 minutes cooking time.
6. Add the brussels sprouts to the Zone 2 basket and return it to the unit.
7. Select the Air fryer mode for Zone 2 with 350 degrees F temperature and 13 minutes cooking time.
8. Press the SMART FINSIH button to sync the settings with Zone 2.
9. Initiate cooking by pressing the START/PAUSE BUTTON.
10. Serve warm and fresh.

Nutritional Information per Serving:

- Calories 405
- Total Fat 22.7 g
- Saturated Fat 6.1 g
- Cholesterol 4 mg
- Sodium 227 mg
- Total Carbs 26.1 g
- Fiber 1.4 g
- Sugar 0.9 g
- Protein 45.2 g

Italian Meatballs

Prep Time: 10 minutes
Cooking Time: 21 minutes
Serving: 6

Ingredients

- 1 medium shallot, minced
- 2 tbsp olive oil
- 3 cloves garlic, minced
- 1/4 cup panko crumbs
- 2 tbsp whole milk
- 2/3 lb lean ground beef
- 1/3 lb bulk turkey sausage
- 1 large egg, lightly beaten
- ¼ cup parsley, chopped
- 1 tbsp fresh thyme, chopped
- 1 tbsp fresh rosemary, chopped
- 1 tbsp Dijon mustard
- ½ tsp salt

Method:

1. At 400 F, preheat your oven. Place a medium non-stick pan over medium-high heat.
2. Add oil and shallot, then sauté for 2 minutes.
3. Toss in garlic and cook for 1 minute.
4. Remove this pan from the heat.
5. Whisk panko with milk in a large bowl and leave it for 5 minutes.
6. Add cooked shallot mixture and mix well.
7. Stir in egg, parsley, turkey sausage, beef, thyme, rosemary, salt, and mustard.
8. Mix well, then divide the mixture into 1 ½ inches balls.
9. Divide these balls in the two Air fryer baskets and spray them with cooking oil.
10. Return the Air Fryer Baskets to the Air Fryer.
11. Select the Air Fryer mode for Zone 1 with 400 degrees F temperature and 21 minutes cooking time.
12. Press the MATCH COOK button to copy the settings for Zone 2.
13. Initiate cooking by pressing the START/PAUSE BUTTON.
14. Serve warm.

Nutritional Information per Serving:

- Calories 545
- Total Fat 36.4 g
- Saturated Fat 10.1 g
- Cholesterol 200 mg

- Sodium 272 mg
- Total Carbs 40.7 g
- Fiber 0.2 g
- Sugar 0.1 g
- Protein 42.5 g

Pork Chops with Broccoli Florets

Prep Time: 10 minutes
Cooking Time: 13 minutes
Serving: 4

Ingredients

- 2 (5 ounce) bone-in pork chops
- 2 tablespoons avocado oil
- 1/2 teaspoon paprika
- 1/2 teaspoon onion powder
- ½ teaspoon garlic powder
- 1 teaspoon salt, divided
- 2 cups broccoli florets
- 2 garlic cloves, minced

Method:

1. Rub the pork chops with avocado oil, garlic, paprika, and spices.
2. Add pork chop to the Zone 1 basket of the Air fryer.
3. Return the Air Fryer Basket to the Air Fryer.
4. Select the Air Fryer mode for Zone 1 with 400 degrees F temperature and 12 minutes cooking time.
5. Add the broccoli to the Zone 2 basket and return it to the unit.
6. Select the Air fryer mode for Zone 2 with 375 degrees F temperature and 13 minutes cooking time.
7. Press the SMART FINSIH button to sync the settings with Zone 2.
8. Initiate cooking by pressing the START/PAUSE BUTTON.
9. Flip the pork once cooked halfway through.
10. Cut the hardened butter into the cubes and place them on top of the pork chops.
11. Serve warm with crispy broccoli florets.

Nutritional Information per Serving:

- Calories 355
- Total Fat 17.5 g
- Saturated Fat 4.8 g
- Cholesterol 283 mg
- Sodium 355 mg
- Total Carbs 26.4 g
- Fiber 1.8 g
- Sugar 0.8 g
- Protein 57.4 g

Parmesan Pork Chops

Prep Time: 10 minutes
Cooking Time: 15 minutes
Serving: 4

Ingredients

- 4 boneless pork chops
- 2 tbsp extra-virgin olive oil
- ½ cup freshly grated Parmesan
- 1 tsp salt
- 1 tsp paprika
- 1 tsp garlic powder
- 1 tsp onion powder
- ½ tsp ground black pepper

Method:

1. Pat dry the pork chops with a paper towel and rub them with olive oil.
2. Mix parmesan with spices in a medium bowl.
3. Rub the pork chops with Parmesan mixture.
4. Place 2 seasoned pork chops in each of the two Air Fryer baskets
5. Return the Air Fryer Baskets to the Air Fryer.
6. Select the Air Fryer mode for Zone 1 with 390 degrees F temperature and 15 minutes cooking time.
7. Press the MATCH COOK button to copy the settings for Zone 2.
8. Initiate cooking by pressing the START/PAUSE BUTTON.
9. Flip the pork chops when cooked halfway through, then resume cooking.
10. Serve warm.

Nutritional Information per Serving:

- Calories 301
- Total Fat 8.9 g
- Saturated Fat 4.5 g
- Cholesterol 57 mg
- Sodium 340 mg
- Total Carbs 24.7 g
- Fiber 1.2 g
- Sugar 1.3 g
- Protein 15.3 g

Beef Cheeseburgers

Prep Time: 10 minutes
Cooking Time: 13 minutes
Serving: 4

Ingredients

- 1 lb ground beef
- Salt, to taste
- 2 cloves garlic, minced
- 1 tbsp soy sauce
- Black pepper, to taste
- 4 American cheese slices
- 4 hamburger buns
- Mayonnaise, to serve
- Lettuce, to serve
- Sliced tomatoes, to serve
- Thinly sliced red onion, to serve

Method:

1. Mix beef with soy sauce, and garlic in a large bowl.
2. Make 4 patties of 4 inches of diameter.
3. Rub them with salt and black pepper on both sides.
4. Place the 2 patties in each of the Air Fryer baskets.
5. Return the Air Fryer Baskets to the Air Fryer.
6. Select the Air Fryer mode for Zone 1 with 390 degrees F temperature and 13 minutes cooking time.
7. Press the MATCH COOK button to copy the settings for Zone 2.
8. Initiate cooking by pressing the START/PAUSE BUTTON.
9. Flip each patty once cooked halfway through, and resume cooking.
10. Add each patty in the hamburger buns along with mayo, tomatoes, onions, and lettuce.
11. Serve.

Nutritional Information per Serving:

- Calories 548
- Total Fat 22.9 g
- Saturated Fat 9 g
- Cholesterol 105 mg
- Sodium 350 mg
- Total Carbs 17.5 g
- Sugar 10.9 g
- Fiber 6.3 g
- Protein 40.1 g

Lamb Shank with Mushroom Stir Fry

Prep Time: 10 minutes
Cooking Time: 35 minutes
Serving: 4

Ingredients

- 20 mushrooms, chopped
- 2 red bell pepper, chopped
- 2 red onion, chopped
- 1 cup red wine
- 4 leeks, chopped
- 6 tbsp balsamic vinegar
- 2 tsp black pepper
- 2 tsp salt
- 3 tbsp fresh rosemary
- 6 cloves garlic
- 4 lamb shanks
- 3 tbsp olive oil

Method:

1. Season the lamb shanks with salt, pepper, rosemary, and 1 tsp olive oil.
2. Set half of the shanks in each of the Air Fryer baskets.
3. Return the Air Fryer Baskets to the Air Fryer.
4. Select the Air Fryer mode for Zone 1 with 390 degrees F temperature and 25 minutes cooking time.
5. Press the MATCH COOK button to copy the settings for Zone 2.
6. Initiate cooking by pressing the START/PAUSE BUTTON.
7. Flip the shanks halfway through, and resume cooking.
8. Meanwhile, add and heat the remaining olive oil in a skillet.
9. Add onion and garlic to sauté for 5 minutes.
10. Add in mushrooms and cook for 5 minutes.
11. Add red wine and cook until it is absorbed
12. Stir all the remaining vegetables along with black pepper and salt.
13. Cook until vegetables are al dente.
14. Serve the air fried shanks with sautéed vegetable fry.

Nutritional Information per Serving:

- Calories 609
- Total Fat 50.5 g
- Saturated Fat 11.7 g
- Cholesterol 58 mg
- Sodium 463 mg
- Total Carbs 9.9 g
- Fiber 1.5 g
- Sugar 0.3 g
- Protein 29.3 g

Korean Brisket

Prep Time: 10 minutes
Cooking Time: 35 minutes
Serving: 4

Ingredients

- ½ tbsp sweet paprika
- ½ tsp toasted sesame oil
- 2 lbs beef brisket, cut into 4 pieces
- Kosher salt, to taste
- 1/8 cup Gochujang, Korean chili paste
- Ground black pepper, to taste
- 1 small onion, diced
- 2 garlic cloves, minced
- 1 tsp Asian fish sauce
- 1 ½ tbsp peanut oil, as needed
- ½ tbsp grated peeled fresh ginger
- ¼ tsp red chili flakes
- ½ cup of water
- 1 tbsp sugar-free ketchup
- 1 tbsp soy sauce

Method:

1. Thoroughly rub the beef brisket with olive oil, paprika, chili flakes, black pepper, and salt.
2. Divide the beef in the two Air Fryer baskets.
3. Return the Air Fryer Baskets to the Air Fryer.
4. Select the Air Fryer mode for Zone 1 with 390 degrees F temperature and 35 minutes cooking time.
5. Press the MATCH COOK button to copy the settings for Zone 2.
6. Initiate cooking by pressing the START/PAUSE BUTTON.
7. Flip the brisket halfway through, and resume cooking.
8. Meanwhile, heat oil in a skillet and add ginger, onion, and garlic.
9. Sauté for 5 minutes, then add all the remaining ingredients.
10. Cook the mixture for 15 minutes approximately until well thoroughly mixed.
11. Serve the brisket with this sauce on top.

Nutritional Information per Serving:

- Calories 537
- Total Fat 19.8 g
- Saturated Fat 1.4 g
- Cholesterol 10 mg
- Sodium 719 mg
- Total Carbs 25.1 g
- Fiber 0.9 g
- Sugar 1.4 g
- Protein 37.8 g

Beef Bites with Chipotle Dip

Prep Time: 10 minutes
Cooking Time: 18 minutes
Serving: 4

Ingredients

- 1 lb beef steak, cut into chunks
- 1 large egg
- Palm oil for frying
- 1/2 cup parmesan cheese, grated
- 1/2 cup pork panko
- 1/2 tsp seasoned salt

Chipotle Ranch Dip

- 1/4 cup mayonnaise
- 1/4 cup sour cream
- 1 tsp chipotle paste
- 1/2 tsp ranch dressing mix
- 1/4 medium lime, juiced

Method:

1. Mix all the ingredients for chipotle ranch dip in a bowl.
2. Keep it in the refrigerator for 30 minutes.
3. Mix pork panko with salt and parmesan.
4. Beat egg in one bowl and spread the panko mixture in another flat bowl.
5. Dip the steak chunks in the egg first then coat them with panko mixture.
6. Spread them in the two Air fryer baskets and spray them with cooking oil.
7. Return the Air Fryer Baskets to the Air Fryer.
8. Select the Air Fryer mode for Zone 1 with 390 degrees F temperature and 18 minutes cooking time.
9. Press the MATCH COOK button to copy the settings for Zone 2.
10. Initiate cooking by pressing the START/PAUSE BUTTON.
11. Serve with chipotle ranch and salt and pepper on top. Enjoy.

Nutritional Information per Serving:

- Calories 452
- Total Fat 4 g
- Saturated Fat 2 g
- Cholesterol 65 mg
- Sodium 220 mg
- Total Carbs 23.1 g
- Fiber 0.3 g
- Sugar 1 g
- Protein 26g

Vegetable Pork Skewers

Prep Time: 10 minutes
Cooking Time: 23 minutes
Serving: 6

Ingredients

- 1 large zucchini, cut 1" pieces
- 1 lb boneless pork belly, cut into cubes
- 1 onion yellow, diced in squares
- 1 ½ cup grape tomatoes
- 1 garlic clove minced
- 1 lemon, juice only
- 1/4 cup olive oil
- 2 tbsp balsamic vinegar
- 1 tsp oregano
- olive oil spray

Method:

1. Mix together balsamic vinegar, garlic, oregano lemon juice, and 1/4 cup olive oil in a suitable bowl.
2. then toss in diced pork pieces and mix well to coat.
3. Leave the seasoned pork to marinate for 60 minutes in the refrigerator.
4. Take suitable wooden skewers for your Air Fryer's Basket, and then thread marinated pork and vegetables on each skewer in an alternating manner.
5. Place half of the skewers in each of the Air fryer basket and spray them with cooking oil.
6. Return the Air Fryer Baskets to the Air Fryer.
7. Select the Air Fryer mode for Zone 1 with 390 degrees F temperature and 23 minutes cooking time.
8. Press the MATCH COOK button to copy the settings for Zone 2.
9. Initiate cooking by pressing the START/PAUSE BUTTON.
10. Flip the skewers once cooked halfway through, and resume cooking.
11. Serve warm.

Nutritional Information per Serving:

- Calories 301
- Total Fat 15.8 g
- Saturated Fat 2.7 g
- Cholesterol 75 mg
- Sodium 389 mg
- Total Carbs 11.7 g
- Fiber 0.3g
- Sugar 0.1 g
- Protein 28.2 g

Dijon Lamb Chops

Prep Time: 10 minutes
Cooking Time: 27 minutes
Serving: 4

Ingredients

- 1 teaspoon Dijon mustard
- 1 teaspoon olive oil
- ½ teaspoon soy sauce
- ½ teaspoon garlic, minced
- ½ teaspoon cumin powder
- ½ teaspoon cayenne pepper
- ½ teaspoon Italian spice blend
- 1/8 teaspoon salt
- 4 pieces of lamb chops

Method:

1. Mix Dijon mustard, soy sauce, olive oil, garlic, cumin powder, cayenne pepper, Italian spice blend, and salt, in a medium bowl and mix well.
2. Place lamb chops into a Ziploc bag and pour in the marinade.
3. Press the air out of the bag and seal tightly.
4. Press the marinade around the lamb chops to fully coat.
5. Keep then in the fridge and marinate for at least 30 minutes, up to overnight.
6. Place 2 chops in each of the Air fryer basket and spray them cooking oil.
7. Return the Air Fryer Baskets to the Air Fryer.
8. Select the Roast mode for Zone 1 with 350 degrees F temperature and 27 minutes cooking time.
9. Press the MATCH COOK button to copy the settings for Zone 2.
10. Initiate cooking by pressing the START/PAUSE BUTTON.
11. Flip the chops once cooked halfway through, and resume cooking.
12. Switch the Air fryer to AIR broil mode and cook for 5 minutes.
13. Serve warm.

Nutritional Information per Serving:

- Calories 308
- Total Fat 20.5 g
- Saturated Fat 3 g
- Cholesterol 42 mg
- Sodium 688 mg
- Total Carbs 40.3 g
- Sugar 1.4 g
- Fiber 4.3 g
- Protein 49 g

Beef-Pepper Kabobs

Prep Time: 10 minutes
Cooking Time: 20 minutes
Serving: 8

Ingredients

- 1 lb beef chuck, stew meat, cubed
- 1/3 cup low fat sour cream
- 2 tbsp soy sauce
- 8 (6-inch) skewers
- 1 bell peppers, squared
- 1/2 onion, squared
- Salt and black pepper, to taste

Method:

1. Whisk sour cream with soy sauce in a medium bowl then toss in beef chunks.
2. Mix well then cover to refrigerate for 30 minutes.
3. Thread the beef, onion, and bell peppers over the skewers alternately.
4. Drizzle the salt and black pepper over the skewers.
5. Place half of the skewers in each of the Air Fryer basket and spray them with cooking oil.
6. Return the Air Fryer Baskets to the Air Fryer.
7. Select the Roast mode for Zone 1 with 390 degrees F temperature and 20 minutes cooking time.
8. Press the MATCH COOK button to copy the settings for Zone 2.
9. Initiate cooking by pressing the START/PAUSE BUTTON.
10. Flip the skewers once cooked halfway through, and resume cooking.
11. Serve warm.

Nutritional Information per Serving:

- Calories 231
- Total Fat 20.1 g
- Saturated Fat 2.4 g
- Cholesterol 110 mg
- Sodium 941 mg
- Total Carbs 20.1 g
- Fiber 0.9 g
- Sugar 1.4 g
- Protein 34.6 g

Sriracha Steak Skewers

Prep Time: 10 minutes
Cooking Time: 28 minutes
Serving: 4

Ingredients

- 1 pound lean steak, cubed
- 2 cups mix vegetables, sliced
- 1/2 cup soy sauce
- 1/2 cup Worcestershire sauce
- 1/4 cup olive oil
- 1/4 cup light brown sugar
- 2 tablespoons spicy mustard
- 1 tablespoon pink Himalayan salt
- 1 tablespoon sesame oil
- 1 teaspoon sriracha
- 1 teaspoon red pepper flakes

Method:

1. Whisk all the ingredients except the beef in a large bowl to prepare the marinade.
2. Toss in the beef cubes and vegetables mix well to coat.
3. Cover the saucy beef mixture and refrigerate to marinate for 2 hours approximately.
4. Start threading the veggies and beef alternately on the wooden skewers.
5. Place these veggie-beef skewers in each of the Air Fryer baskets and spray them with cooking oil.
6. Return the Air Fryer Baskets to the Air Fryer.
7. Select the Roast mode for Zone 1 with 390 degrees F temperature and 28 minutes cooking time.
8. Press the MATCH COOK button to copy the settings for Zone 2.
9. Initiate cooking by pressing the START/PAUSE BUTTON.
10. Flip the skewers once cooked halfway through, and resume cooking.
11. Serve warm.

Nutritional Information per Serving:

- Calories 472
- Total Fat 11.1 g
- Saturated Fat 5.8 g
- Cholesterol 610 mg
- Sodium 749 mg
- Total Carbs 19.9 g
- Fiber 0.2 g
- Sugar 0.2 g
- Protein 23.5 g

Pork Pineapple Skewers

Prep Time: 10 minutes
Cooking Time: 23 minutes
Serving: 8

Ingredients

- 4 thick-cut boneless pork chops, cut into chunks
- 2 fresh pineapple, cut into chunks
- 2 tbsp of chopped fresh parsley
- 8 skewers

Method:

1. Thread the pineapple and pork chunks over the wooden skewers.
2. Divide these skewers in the two Air Fryer baskets and spray them with cooking oil.
3. Return the Air Fryer Baskets to the Air Fryer.
4. Select the Roast mode for Zone 1 with 390 degrees F temperature and 23 minutes cooking time.
5. Press the MATCH COOK button to copy the settings for Zone 2.
6. Initiate cooking by pressing the START/PAUSE BUTTON.
7. Flip the skewers once cooked half through and resume cooking.
8. Serve warm.

Nutritional Information per Serving:

- Calories 327
- Total Fat 3.5 g
- Saturated Fat 0.5 g
- Cholesterol 162 mg
- Sodium 142 mg
- Total Carbs 33.6 g
- Fiber 0.4 g
- Sugar 0.5 g
- Protein 24.5 g

Pork Skewers with Mango Salsa

Prep Time: 10 minutes
Cooking Time: 18 minutes
Serving: 4

Ingredients

- 2 tablespoons white sugar
- 4 1/2 teaspoons onion powder
- 4 1/2 teaspoons dried thyme, crushed
- 1 tablespoon ground allspice
- 1 tablespoon ground black pepper
- 1 1/2 teaspoons cayenne pepper, or to taste
- 1 1/2 teaspoons salt
- 3/4 teaspoon ground nutmeg
- 1/4 teaspoon ground cloves
- 1/4 cup shredded coconut
- 1 (1 pound) pork tenderloin, cubed
- 4 bamboo skewers, soaked, drained
- 1 tablespoon vegetable oil
- 1 mango - peeled, seeded, and chopped
- 1/2 (15 oz.) can black beans, rinsed and drained
- 1/4 cup finely chopped red onion
- 2 tablespoons fresh lime juice
- 1 tablespoon honey
- 1 tablespoon chopped fresh cilantro
- 1/4 teaspoon salt
- 1/8 teaspoon ground black pepper

Method:

1. Start by mixing sugar, thyme, onion powder, black pepper, allspice, salt, nutmeg, cloves, and cayenne pepper in a bowl.
2. Take one 1 tbsp of this seasoning in a bowl and preserve the rest in an airtight container.
3. Add coconut to this 1 tbsp seasoning and mix it well.
4. Stir in the pork chunks and toss well to coat them with the seasoning.
5. Thread the pork meat over the wooden skewers.
6. Place half of these skewers in each of the Air Fryer baskets and spray them with cooking oil.
7. Return the Air Fryer Baskets to the Air Fryer.
8. Select the Air Fryer mode for Zone 1 with 350 degrees F temperature and 18 minutes cooking time.
9. Press the MATCH COOK button to copy the settings for Zone 2.
10. Initiate cooking by pressing the START/PAUSE BUTTON.
11. During this time, mix mango, onion and all remaining ingredients in a salad bowl.

12. Serve the pork skewers with mango salsa.
13. Enjoy.

Nutritional Information per Serving:

- Calories 353
- Total Fat 7.5 g
- Saturated Fat 1.1 g
- Cholesterol 20 mg
- Sodium 297 mg
- Total Carbs 10.4 g
- Fiber 0.2 g
- Sugar 0.1 g
- Protein 33.1 g

Chapter 6: Poultry

Chicken Katsu

Prep Time: 10 minutes
Cooking Time: 26 minutes
Serving: 2

Ingredients

- 1 lb boneless chicken breast, cut in half
- 2 large eggs, beaten
- 1 ½ cups panko bread crumbs
- Salt and black pepper ground to taste
- Cooking spray

Sauce:

- 1 tbsp sugar
- 2 tbsp soy sauce
- 1 tbsp sherry
- ½ cup ketchup
- 2 tsp Worcestershire sauce
- 1 tsp minced garlic

Method:

1. Mix soy sauce, ketchup, sherry, sugar, garlic and Worcestershire sauce in a mixing bowl.
2. Keep this katsu aside for a while.
3. Rub the chicken pieces with salt and black pepper.
4. Whisk eggs in a shallow dish and spread breadcrumbs in another tray.
5. Dip the chicken in the eggs mixture and coat them with breadcrumbs.
6. Place the coated chicken in the two Air Fryer Baskets and spray them with cooking spray.
7. Return the Air Fryer Baskets to the Air Fryer.
8. Select the Air Fryer mode for Zone 1 with 390 degrees F temperature and 26 minutes cooking time.
9. Press the MATCH COOK button to copy the settings for Zone 2.
10. Initiate cooking by pressing the START/PAUSE BUTTON.
11. Flip the chicken once cooked halfway through, then resume cooking.
12. Serve warm with the sauce.

Nutritional Information per Serving:

- Calories 248
- Total Fat 13 g

- Saturated Fat 7 g
- Cholesterol 387 mg
- Sodium 353 mg
- Total Carbs 1 g
- Fiber 0.4 g
- Sugar 1 g
- Protein 29 g

Bacon-Wrapped Chicken Thighs

Prep Time: 10 minutes
Cooking Time: 28 minutes
Serving: 8

Ingredients

Butter:

- ½ stick butter, softened
- ½ clove minced garlic
- ¼ tsp dried thyme
- ¼ tsp dried basil
- ⅛ tsp coarse salt
- 1 pinch black pepper, ground
- ⅓ lb thick-cut bacon
- 1 ½ lbs boneless skinless chicken thighs
- 2 tsp minced garlic

Method:

1. Mix garlic, softened butter, with thyme, salt, basil, and black pepper in a bowl.
2. Add butter mixture on a piece of wax paper and roll it up tightly to make a butter log.
3. Place the log in the refrigerator for 2 hours.
4. Spray one bacon strip on a piece of wax paper.
5. Place each chicken thigh on top of one bacon strip and rub it with garlic.
6. Make a slit in the chicken thigh and add a tsp of butter to the chicken.
7. Wrap the bacon around the chicken thigh.
8. Repeat those same steps with all the chicken thighs.
9. Place the bacon wrapped chicken thighs in the two Air Fryer Baskets.
10. Return the Air Fryer Baskets to the Air Fryer.
11. Select the Air Fryer mode for Zone 1 with 390 degrees F temperature and 28 minutes cooking time.
12. Press the MATCH COOK button to copy the settings for Zone 2.
13. Initiate cooking by pressing the START/PAUSE BUTTON.
14. Flip the chicken once cooked halfway through, and resume cooking.
15. Serve warm.

Nutritional Information per Serving:

- Calories 457
- Total Fat 19.1 g
- Saturated Fat 11 g
- Cholesterol 262 mg

- Sodium 557 mg
- Total Carbs 18.9 g
- Sugar 1.2 g
- Fiber 1.7 g
- Protein 32.5 g

Bang-Bang Chicken

Prep Time: 10 minutes
Cooking Time: 20 minutes
Serving: 2

Ingredients

- 1 cup mayonnaise
- ½ cup sweet chili sauce
- 2 tbsp Sriracha sauce
- ⅓ cup flour
- 1 lb boneless chicken breast, diced
- 1 ½ cups panko bread crumbs
- 2 green onions, chopped

Method:

1. Mix mayonnaise with Sriracha and sweet chili sauce in a large bowl.
2. Keep 3/4 cup of the mixture aside.
3. Add flour, chicken, breadcrumbs and remaining mayo mixture to a resealable plastic bag.
4. Zip the bag and shake well to coat.
5. Divide the chicken in the two Air fryer baskets in a single layer.
6. Return the Air Fryer Baskets to the Air Fryer.
7. Select the Air Fryer mode for Zone 1 with 390 degrees F temperature and 20 minutes cooking time.
8. Press the MATCH COOK button to copy the settings for Zone 2.
9. Initiate cooking by pressing the START/PAUSE BUTTON.
10. Flip the chicken once cooked halfway through.
11. Top the chicken with reserved mayo sauce.
12. Garnish with green onions and serve warm.

Nutritional Information per Serving:

- Calories 392
- Total Fat 16.1 g
- Saturated Fat 2.3 g
- Cholesterol 231 mg
- Sodium 466 mg
- Total Carbs 3.9 g
- Sugar 0.6 g
- Fiber 0.9 g
- Protein 48 g

Tso's Chicken

Prep Time: 10 minutes
Cooking Time: 20 minutes
Serving: 4

Ingredients

- 1 egg, large
- 1 lb boneless, skinless chicken thighs, cut into 1 ¼ -inch chunks
- 1/3 cup 2 tsp cornstarch,
- 1/4 tsp salt
- 1/4 tsp ground white pepper
- 7 tbsp lower-sodium chicken broth
- 2 tbsp lower-sodium soy sauce
- 2 tbsp ketchup
- 2 tsp sugar
- 2 tsp unseasoned rice vinegar
- 1 1/2 tbsp canola oil
- 4 chilies de árbol, chopped and seeds discarded
- 1 tbsp chopped fresh ginger
- 1 tbsp chopped garlic
- 2 tbsp green onion, thinly sliced
- 1 tsp toasted sesame oil
- 1/2 tsp toasted sesame seeds

Method:

1. Add egg to a large bowl and beat it with a fork.
2. Add chicken to the egg and coat it well.
3. Whisk 1/3 cup cornstarch with black pepper and salt in a small bowl.
4. Add chicken to the cornstarch mixture and mix well to coat.
5. Divide the chicken in the two air fryer baskets and spray them cooking oi.
6. Return the Air Fryer Baskets to the Air Fryer.
7. Select the Air Fryer mode for Zone 1 with 390 degrees F temperature and 20 minutes cooking time.
8. Press the MATCH COOK button to copy the settings for Zone 2.
9. Initiate cooking by pressing the START/PAUSE BUTTON.
10. Once done, remove the air fried chicken from the Air fryer.
11. Whisk 2 tsp cornstarch with soy sauce, broth, sugar, ketchup, and rice vinegar in a small bowl.
12. Add chilies and canola oil to a skillet and sauté for 1 minute.
13. Add garlic and ginger then sauté for 30 seconds.
14. Stir in cornstarch sauce and cook until it bubbles and thickens.

15. Toss in cooked chicken and garnish with sesame oil, sesame seeds, and green onion.
16. Enjoy.

Nutritional Information per Serving:

- Calories 321
- Total Fat 7.4 g
- Saturated Fat 4.6 g
- Cholesterol 105 mg
- Sodium 353 mg
- Total Carbs 19.4 g
- Sugar 6.5 g
- Fiber 2.7 g
- Protein 37.2 g

Chicken Wing Drumettes

Prep Time: 10 minutes
Cooking Time: 47 minutes
Serving: 5

Ingredients

- 10 large chicken drumettes
- Cooking spray
- ¼ cup of rice vinegar
- 3 tbsp honey
- 2 tbsp unsalted chicken stock
- 1 tbsp lower-sodium soy sauce
- 1 tbsp toasted sesame oil
- 3/8 tsp crushed red pepper
- 1 garlic clove, chopped
- 2 tbsp chopped unsalted roasted peanuts
- 1 tbsp chopped fresh chives

Method:

1. Spread the chicken in the two Air Fryer Baskets in an even layer and spray cooking spray on top.
2. Return the Air Fryer Baskets to the Air Fryer.
3. Select the Air Fryer mode for Zone 1 with 390 degrees F temperature and 47 minutes cooking time.
4. Press the MATCH COOK button to copy the settings for Zone 2.
5. Initiate cooking by pressing the START/PAUSE BUTTON.
6. Flip the chicken drumettes once cooked halfway through, then resume cooking.
7. During this time, mix soy sauce, honey, stock, vinegar, garlic, and crushed red pepper in a suitable saucepan and place it over medium-high heat to cook on a simmer.
8. Cook this sauce for 6 minutes with occasional stirring then pour it into a medium-sized bowl.
9. Add Air fried drumettes and toss well to coat with the honey sauce.
10. Garnish with chives and peanuts.
11. Serve warm and fresh.

Nutritional Information per Serving:

- Calories 248
- Total Fat 15.7 g
- Saturated Fat 2.7 g
- Cholesterol 75 mg
- Sodium 94 mg
- Total Carbs 31.4 g
- Fiber 0.4 g
- Sugar 3.1 g
- Protein 24.9 g

Crusted Chicken Breast

Prep Time: 10 minutes
Cooking Time: 28 minutes
Serving: 4

Ingredients

- 2 large eggs, beaten
- 1/2 cup all-purpose flour
- 1 1/4 cup panko bread crumbs
- 2/3 cup Parmesan, grated
- 4 tsp lemon zest
- 2 tsp dried oregano
- Salt, to taste
- 1 tsp cayenne pepper
- Freshly ground black pepper, to taste
- 4 boneless skinless chicken breasts

Method:

1. Beat eggs in one shallow bowl and spread flour in another shallow bowl.
2. Mix panko with oregano, lemon zest, Parmesan, cayenne, oregano, salt, and black pepper in another shallow bowl.
3. First coat the chicken with flour first, then dip it in the eggs and coat them with panko mixture.
4. Arrange the prepared chicken in the two Air Fryer Baskets.
5. Return the Air Fryer Baskets to the Air Fryer.
6. Select the Air Fryer mode for Zone 1 with 390 degrees F temperature and 28 minutes cooking time.
7. Press the MATCH COOK button to copy the settings for Zone 2.
8. Initiate cooking by pressing the START/PAUSE BUTTON.
9. Flip the half-cooked chicken and continue cooking for 5 minutes until golden.
10. Serve warm.

Nutritional Information per Serving:

- Calories 378
- Total Fat 21 g
- Saturated Fat 4.3 g
- Cholesterol 150 mg
- Sodium 146 mg
- Total Carbs 7.1 g
- Sugar 0.1 g
- Fiber 0.4 g
- Protein 23 g

Crispy Chicken Fillets

Prep Time: 10 minutes
Cooking Time: 28 minutes
Serving: 4

Ingredients

- 2 boneless chicken breasts
- 1/2 cup dill pickle juice
- 2 eggs
- 1/2 cup milk
- 1 cup flour, all-purpose
- 2 tbsp powdered sugar
- 2 tbsp potato starch
- 1 tsp paprika
- 1 tsp of sea salt
- 1/2 tsp black pepper
- 1/2 tsp garlic powder
- 1/4 tsp ground celery seed ground
- 1 tbsp extra virgin olive oil
- Cooking spray
- 4 hamburger buns, toasted
- 8 dill pickle chips

Method:

1. Set the chicken in a suitable Ziplock bag and pound it into ½ thickness with a mallet.
2. Slice the chicken into 2 halves.
3. Add pickle juice and seal the bag.
4. Refrigerate for 30 minutes approximately for marination. Whisk both eggs with milk in a shallow bowl.
5. Thoroughly mix flour with spices and flour in a separate bowl.
6. Dip each chicken slice in egg then in the flour mixture.
7. Shake off the excess and set the chicken pieces in the Air Fryer basket.
8. Spray the pieces with cooking oil.
9. Place the chicken pieces in the two air fryer baskets in a single layer and spray them cooking oil.
10. Return the Air Fryer Baskets to the Air Fryer.
11. Select the Air Fryer mode for Zone 1 with 390 degrees F temperature and 28 minutes cooking time.
12. Press the MATCH COOK button to copy the settings for Zone 2.
13. Initiate cooking by pressing the START/PAUSE BUTTON.
14. Flip the chicken pieces once cooked halfway through, and resume cooking.
15. Enjoy with pickle chips and a dollop of mayonnaise.

Nutritional Information per Serving:

- Calories 351
- Total Fat 4 g
- Saturated Fat 6.3 g
- Cholesterol 360 mg
- Sodium 236 mg
- Total Carbs 19.1 g
- Sugar 0.3 g
- Fiber 0.1 g
- Protein 36 g

Chicken Potatoes Mix

Prep Time: 10 minutes
Cooking Time: 22 minutes
Serving: 4

Ingredients

- 15 oz canned potatoes drained
- 1 tsp olive oil
- 1 tsp Lawry's seasoned salt
- 1/8 tsp black pepper optional
- 8 oz boneless skinless chicken breast cubed
- 1/4 tsp paprika optional
- 3/8 cup cheddar, shredded
- 4 slices bacon, cooked, cut into strips

Method:

1. Dice the chicken into small pieces and toss them with olive oil and spices.
2. Drain and dice the potato pieces into smaller cubes.
3. Add potato to the chicken and mix well to coat.
4. Spread the mixture in the two Air fryer baskets in a single layer.
5. Return the Air Fryer Baskets to the Air Fryer.
6. Select the Air Fryer mode for Zone 1 with 390 degrees F temperature and 22 minutes cooking time.
7. Press the MATCH COOK button to copy the settings for Zone 2.
8. Initiate cooking by pressing the START/PAUSE BUTTON.
9. Top the chicken and potatoes with cheese and bacon.
10. Return the Air Fryer Baskets to the Air Fryer.
11. Select the Air Broil mode for Zone 1 with 300 degrees F temperature and 5 minutes cooking time.
12. Initiate cooking by pressing the START/PAUSE BUTTON.
13. Repeat the same step for ZONE 2 to broil the potatoes and chicken in the 2nd basket.
14. Enjoy with dried herbs on top.

Nutritional Information per Serving:

- Calories 378
- Total Fat 7 g
- Saturated Fat 8.1 g
- Cholesterol 230 mg
- Sodium 316 mg
- Total Carbs 16.2 g
- Sugar 0.2 g
- Fiber 0.3 g
- Protein 26 g

Air Fried Turkey Breast

Prep Time: 10 minutes
Cooking Time: 46 minutes
Serving: 4

Ingredients

- 2 lb turkey breast, on the bone with skin
- ½ tbsp olive oil
- 1 tsp kosher salt
- 1/4 tbsp dry poultry seasoning

Method:

1. Rub turkey breast with ½ tbsp oil.
2. Season both its sides with turkey seasoning and salt, then rub in the brush half tbsp of oil over the skin of the turkey.
3. Divide the turkey in half and place each half in each of the Air fryer baskets.
4. Return the Air Fryer Baskets to the Air Fryer.
5. Select the Air Fryer mode for Zone 1 with 390 degrees F temperature and 46 minutes cooking time.
6. Press the MATCH COOK button to copy the settings for Zone 2.
7. Initiate cooking by pressing the START/PAUSE BUTTON.
8. Flip the turkey once cooked halfway through, and resume cooking.
9. Slice and serve warm.

Nutritional Information per Serving:

- Calories 246
- Total Fat 14.8 g
- Saturated Fat 0.7 g
- Cholesterol 22 mg
- Sodium 220 mg
- Total Carbs 40.3 g
- Fiber 2.4 g
- Sugar 1.2 g
- Protein 42.4 g

Chili Chicken Wings

Prep Time: 10 minutes
Cooking Time: 43 minutes
Serving: 4

Ingredients

- 8 chicken wings drumettes
- cooking spray
- 1/8 cup low-fat buttermilk
- 1/4 cup almond flour
- McCormick Chicken Seasoning to taste

Thai Chili Marinade

- 1 1/2 tbsp low-sodium soy sauce
- ½ tsp ginger, minced
- 1 1/2 garlic cloves
- 1 green onion
- ½ tsp rice wine vinegar
- ½ tbsp Sriracha sauce
- ½ tbsp sesame oil

Method:

1. Put all the ingredients for the marinade in the blender and blend them for 1 minute.
2. Keep this marinade aside. Pat dry the washed chicken and place it in the Ziploc bag.
3. Add buttermilk, chicken seasoning, and zip the bag.
4. Shake the bag well then refrigerator for 30 minutes for marination.
5. Remove the chicken drumettes from the marinade then dredge it through dry flour.
6. Spread the drumettes in the two air fryer baskets and spray them with cooking oil.
7. Return the Air Fryer Baskets to the Air Fryer.
8. Select the Air Fryer mode for Zone 1 with 390 degrees F temperature and 43 minutes cooking time.
9. Press the MATCH COOK button to copy the settings for Zone 2.
10. Initiate cooking by pressing the START/PAUSE BUTTON.
11. Toss the drumettes once cooked halfway through.
12. Now brush the chicken pieces with Thai chili sauce and then resume cooking
13. Serve warm.

Nutritional Information per Serving:

- Calories 338
- Total Fat 23.8 g
- Saturated Fat 0.7 g
- Cholesterol 22 mg
- Sodium 620 mg
- Total Carbs 8.3 g
- Fiber 2.4 g
- Sugar 1.2 g
- Protein 45.4 g

Turkey Mushroom Burgers

Prep Time: 10 minutes
Cooking Time: 17 minutes
Serving: 4

Ingredients

- 3 medium mushrooms
- 1/2 tbsp Maggi seasoning sauce
- 1/2 tsp garlic powder
- 1/2 tsp onion powder
- 1/4 tsp salt substitute
- 1/4 tsp ground black pepper
- ½ lb ground turkey

Method:

1. Puree washed mushrooms in a food processor until smooth.
2. Add seasoning sauce, pepper, salt, and onion powder.
3. Mix well, then add this mushroom mixture to the turkey ground.
4. Combine the mixture well then make five patties out of it.
5. Place half of the patties in each of the Air Fryer Baskets and spray them with cooking oil.
6. Return the Air Fryer Baskets to the Air Fryer.
7. Select the Air Fryer mode for Zone 1 with 390 degrees F temperature and 17 minutes cooking time.
8. Press the MATCH COOK button to copy the settings for Zone 2.
9. Initiate cooking by pressing the START/PAUSE BUTTON.
10. Serve warm.

Nutritional Information per Serving:

- Calories 438
- Total Fat 4.8 g
- Saturated Fat 1.7 g
- Cholesterol 12 mg
- Sodium 520 mg
- Total Carbs 58.3 g
- Fiber 2.3 g
- Sugar 1.2 g
- Protein 32.1 g

Brazilian Chicken

Prep Time: 10 minutes
Cooking Time: 47 minutes
Serving: 4

Ingredients

- 2 tsp cumin seeds
- 2 tsp dried parsley
- 2 tsp turmeric powder
- 2 tsp dried oregano leaves
- 2 tsp salt
- 1 tsp coriander seeds
- 1 tsp black peppercorns
- 1 tsp cayenne pepper
- 1/2 cup lime juice
- 4 tbsp vegetable oil
- 3 lbs chicken drumsticks

Method:

1. Grind cumin, parsley, salt, coriander seeds, cayenne pepper, peppercorns, oregano, and turmeric in a food processor.
2. Add this mixture to lemon juice and oil in a bowl and mix well.
3. Rub the spice paste over the chicken drumsticks and let them marinate for 30 minutes.
4. Divide the chicken drumsticks in both the Air Fryer Baskets.
5. Return the Air Fryer Baskets to the Air Fryer.
6. Select the Air Fryer mode for Zone 1 with 390 degrees F temperature and 47 minutes cooking time.
7. Press the MATCH COOK button to copy the settings for Zone 2.
8. Initiate cooking by pressing the START/PAUSE BUTTON.
9. Flip the drumsticks when cooked halfway through, then resume cooking.
10. Serve warm.

Nutritional Information per Serving:

- Calories 378
- Total Fat 3.8 g
- Saturated Fat 0.7 g
- Cholesterol 2 mg
- Sodium 620 mg
- Total Carbs 13.3 g
- Fiber 2.4 g
- Sugar 1.2 g
- Protein 25.4 g

Chapter 7: Seafood and Fish

Spinach Scallops

Prep Time: 10 minutes
Cooking Time: 13 minutes
Serving: 4

Ingredients

- 3/4 cup heavy whipping cream
- 1 tbsp tomato paste
- 1 tbsp chopped fresh basil
- 1 tsp minced garlic
- 1/2 tsp salt
- 1/2 tsp pepper
- 12 oz frozen spinach thawed
- 8 jumbo sea scallops
- Vegetable oil to spray

Method:

1. Season the scallops with vegetable oil, salt, and pepper in a bowl
2. Mix cream with spinach, basil, garlic, salt, pepper, and tomato paste in a bowl.
3. Pour this mixture over the scallops and mix gently.
4. Divide the scallops in the Air Fryers Baskets, without using the crisper plate.
5. Return the Air Fryer Baskets to the Air Fryer.
6. Select the Air Fryer mode for Zone 1 with 390 degrees F temperature and 13 minutes cooking time.
7. Press the MATCH COOK button to copy the settings for Zone 2.
8. Initiate cooking by pressing the START/PAUSE BUTTON.
9. Serve right away.

Nutritional Information per Serving:

- Calories 341
- Total Fat 4 g
- Saturated Fat 0.5 g
- Cholesterol 69 mg
- Sodium 547 mg
- Total Carbs 36.4 g
- Fiber 1.2 g
- Sugar 1 g
- Protein 30.3 g

Fish Finger Sandwich

Prep Time: 10 minutes
Cooking Time: 22 minutes
Serving: 4

Ingredients

- 4 small cod fillets, skinless
- Salt and black pepper, to taste
- 2 tbsp flour
- ¼ cup dried breadcrumbs
- Spray oil
- 9 oz frozen peas
- 1 tbsp creme fraiche
- 12 capers
- 1 squeeze of lemon juice
- 4 bread rolls, cut in halve

Method:

1. First coat the cod fillets with flour, salt and black pepper.
2. Then coat the fish with breadcrumbs.
3. Divide the coated cod fish in the two Air fryer baskets and spray them with cooking spray.
4. Return the Air Fryer Baskets to the Air Fryer.
5. Select the Air Fryer mode for Zone 1 with 390 degrees F temperature and 17 minutes cooking time.
6. Press the MATCH COOK button to copy the settings for Zone 2.
7. Initiate cooking by pressing the START/PAUSE BUTTON.
8. Meanwhile boil peas in hot water for 5 minutes until soft.
9. Then drain the peas and transfer them to the blender.
10. Add capers, lemon juice and crème fraiche to the blender.
11. Blend until it makes smooth mixture.
12. Spread the peas crème mixture on top of 2 lower halves of the bread roll, and place the fish fillets on it.
13. Place the remaining bread slices on top.
14. Serve fresh.

Nutritional Information per Serving:

- Calories 391
- Total Fat 2.2 g
- Saturated Fat 2.4 g
- Cholesterol 10 mg
- Sodium 276 mg
- Total Carbs 7.7 g
- Fiber 0.9 g
- Sugar 1.4 g
- Protein 28.8 g

Lobster Tails

Prep Time: 10 minutes
Cooking Time: 18 minutes
Serving: 4

Ingredients

- 4 (4 oz) lobster tails
- 8 tbsp butter, melted
- 2 tsp lemon zest
- 2 clove garlic, grated
- Salt and black pepper ground to taste
- 2 tsp fresh parsley, chopped
- 4 wedges lemon

Method:

1. Spread the lobster tails into Butterfly, slit the top to expose the lobster meat while keeping the tail intact.
2. Place two lobster tails in each of the Air Fryer baskets with their lobster meat facing up.
3. Mix melted butter with lemon zest and garlic in a bowl.
4. Brush the butter mixture on top of the lobster tails.
5. And drizzle salt and black pepper on top.
6. Return the Air Fryer Baskets to the Air Fryer.
7. Select the Air Fryer mode for Zone 1 with 390 degrees F temperature and 18 minutes cooking time.
8. Press the MATCH COOK button to copy the settings for Zone 2.
9. Initiate cooking by pressing the START/PAUSE BUTTON.
10. Garnish with parsley and lemon wedges.
11. Serve warm.

Nutritional Information per Serving:

- Calories 348
- Total Fat 22.4 g
- Saturated Fat 10.1 g
- Cholesterol 320 mg
- Sodium 350 mg
- Total Carbs 32.2 g
- Fiber 0.7 g
- Sugar 0.7 g
- Protein 41.3 g

Buttered Mahi Mahi

Prep Time: 10 minutes
Cooking Time: 17 minutes
Serving: 4

Ingredients

- 4 (6 oz) mahi mahi fillets
- Salt and black pepper ground to taste
- Cooking spray
- ⅔ cup butter

Method:

1. Preheat your Air Fryer Machine to 350 F.
2. Rub the mahi mahi fillets with salt and black pepper.
3. Place two mahi mahi fillets in each of the Air Fryer's Basket.
4. Return the Air Fryer Baskets to the Air Fryer.
5. Select the Air Fryer mode for Zone 1 with 390 degrees F temperature and 17 minutes cooking time.
6. Press the MATCH COOK button to copy the settings for Zone 2.
7. Initiate cooking by pressing the START/PAUSE BUTTON.
8. Add butter to a saucepan and cook for 5 minutes until slightly brown.
9. Remove the butter from the heat.
10. Drizzle butter over the fish and serve warm.

Nutritional Information per Serving:

- Calories 294
- Total Fat 11.1 g
- Saturated Fat 5.8 g
- Cholesterol 610 mg
- Sodium 749 mg
- Total Carbs 49 g
- Fiber 0.2 g
- Sugar 0.2 g
- Protein 23.5 g

Salmon Fillets with Fennel Salad

Prep Time: 10 minutes
Cooking Time: 17 minutes
Serving: 4

Ingredients

- 2 tsp chopped fresh flat-leaf parsley
- 1 tsp chopped fresh thyme
- 1 tsp salt, divided
- 4 (6-oz) skinless center-cut salmon fillets
- 2 tbsp olive oil
- 4 cups thinly sliced fennel
- 2/3 cup 2% reduced-fat Greek yogurt
- 1 garlic clove, grated
- 2 tbsp orange juice
- 1 tsp lemon juice
- 2 tbsp chopped fresh dill

Method:

1. At 200 F, preheat your Air Fryer.
2. Mix ½ tsp salt, thyme, and parsley in a small bowl.
3. Brush the salmon with oil first, then rub liberally rub the herb mixture.
4. Place 2 salmon fillets in each of the Air fryer basket.
5. Return the Air Fryer Baskets to the Air Fryer.
6. Select the Air Fryer mode for Zone 1 with 390 degrees F temperature and 17 minutes cooking time.
7. Press the MATCH COOK button to copy the settings for Zone 2.
8. Initiate cooking by pressing the START/PAUSE BUTTON.
9. Meanwhile, mix fennel with garlic, yogurt, lemon juice, orange juice, remaining salt, and dill in a mixing bowl.
10. Serve the Air Fried Salmon fillets with fennel salad.
11. Enjoy.

Nutritional Information per Serving:

- Calories 350
- Total Fat 3.5 g
- Saturated Fat 0 g
- Cholesterol 7 mg
- Sodium 94 mg
- Total Carbs 15 g
- Fiber 1 g
- Sugar 1 g
- Protein 32 g

Sweet Salmon Fillets

Prep Time: 10 minutes
Cooking Time: 17 minutes
Serving: 4

Ingredients

- 4 (6-oz) salmon fillets
- Salt
- Freshly ground black pepper
- 4 tsp extra-virgin olive oil
- 4 tbsp wholegrain mustard
- 2 tbsp packed brown sugar
- 2 clove garlic, minced
- 1 tsp thyme leaves

Method:

1. Rub the salmon with salt and black pepper first.
2. Whisk oil with sugar, thyme, garlic, and mustard in a small bowl.
3. Place two salmon fillet in each of the Air Fryer baskets and brush the thyme mixture on top of each fillet.
4. Return the Air Fryer Baskets to the Air Fryer.
5. Select the Air Fryer mode for Zone 1 with 390 degrees F temperature and 17 minutes cooking time.
6. Press the MATCH COOK button to copy the settings for Zone 2.
7. Initiate cooking by pressing the START/PAUSE BUTTON.
8. Serve warm and fresh.

Nutritional Information per Serving:

- Calories 349
- Total Fat 11.9 g
- Saturated Fat 1.7 g
- Cholesterol 78 mg
- Sodium 79 mg
- Total Carbs 12.8 g
- Fiber 1.1 g
- Sugar 20.3 g
- Protein 35 g

Crusted Cod Fish

Prep Time: 10 minutes
Cooking Time: 13 minutes
Serving: 4

Ingredients

- 2 lbs cod fillets
- Salt, to taste
- Freshly ground black pepper, to taste
- ½ cup all-purpose flour
- 1 large egg, beaten
- 2 cups panko bread crumbs
- 1 tsp Old Bay seasoning
- Lemon wedges, for serving
- Tartar sauce, for serving

Method:

1. Rub the fish with salt and black pepper.
2. Add flour in one shallow bowl, beat eggs in another bowl and mix panko with Old Bay in a shallow bowl.
3. First coat the fish with flour, then dip it in the eggs and finally coat with the panko mixture.
4. Place half of the seasoned cod fish in each Air Fryer basket.
5. Return the Air Fryer Baskets to the Air Fryer.
6. Select the Air Fryer mode for Zone 1 with 390 degrees F temperature and 13 minutes cooking time.
7. Press the MATCH COOK button to copy the settings for Zone 2.
8. Initiate cooking by pressing the START/PAUSE BUTTON.
9. Flip the fish once cooked halfway then resume cooking.
10. Serve warm and fresh with tartar sauce and lemon wedges.

Nutritional Information per Serving:

- Calories 413
- Total Fat 4 g
- Saturated Fat 8 g
- Cholesterol 81 mg
- Sodium 162 mg
- Total Carbs 13 g
- Fiber 2.7 g
- Sugar 1 g
- Protein 22 g

Glazed Scallops

Prep Time: 10 minutes
Cooking Time: 13 minutes
Serving: 12

Ingredients

- 12 scallops
- 3 tbsp olive oil
- Black pepper and salt to taste

Method:

1. Rub the scallops with olive oil, black pepper, and salt.
2. Divide the scallops in the two Air fryer baskets.
3. Return the Air Fryer Baskets to the Air Fryer.
4. Select the Air Fryer mode for Zone 1 with 390 degrees F temperature and 13 minutes cooking time.
5. Press the MATCH COOK button to copy the settings for Zone 2.
6. Initiate cooking by pressing the START/PAUSE BUTTON.
7. Flip the scallops once cooked halfway through, and resume cooking.
8. Serve warm.

Nutritional Information per Serving:

- Calories 279
- Total Fat 29.7 g
- Saturated Fat 8.6 g
- Cholesterol 141 mg
- Sodium 193 mg
- Total Carbs 13.7g
- Fiber 0.4 g
- Sugar 1.3 g
- Protein 10.2 g

Crusted Tilapia Fillets

Prep Time: 10 minutes
Cooking Time: 10 minutes
Serving: 4

Ingredients

- 3/4 cup breadcrumbs
- 1 packet dry ranch-style dressing
- 2 1/2 tbsp vegetable oil
- 2 eggs beaten
- 4 tilapia fillets
- Herbs and chilies to garnish

Method:

1. Thoroughly mix ranch dressing with panko in a bowl.
2. Whisk eggs in a shallow bowl.
3. Dip each fish fillet in the egg then coat evenly with the panko mixture.
4. Set two coated fillets in each of the Air Fryer baskets.
5. Return the Air Fryer Baskets to the Air Fryer.
6. Select the Air Fryer mode for Zone 1 with 390 degrees F temperature and 17 minutes cooking time.
7. Press the MATCH COOK button to copy the settings for Zone 2.
8. Initiate cooking by pressing the START/PAUSE BUTTON.
9. Serve warm with herbs and chilies.

Nutritional Information per Serving:

- Calories 368
- Total Fat 6 g
- Saturated Fat 1.2 g
- Cholesterol 351 mg
- Sodium 103 mg
- Total Carbs 72.8 g
- Fiber 9.2 g
- Sugar 32.9 g
- Protein 7.2 g

Crispy Catfish Fillets

Prep Time: 10 minutes
Cooking Time: 17 minutes
Serving: 4

Ingredients

- 4 catfish fillets
- 1/4 cup Louisiana Fish fry
- 1 tbsp olive oil
- 1 tbsp chopped parsley optional
- 1 lemon, sliced
- Fresh herbs, to garnish

Method:

1. Mix fish fry with olive oil, and parsley then liberally rub over the catfish.
2. Place two fillets in each of the Air fryer baskets.
3. Return the Air Fryer Baskets to the Air Fryer.
4. Select the Air Fryer mode for Zone 1 with 390 degrees F temperature and 17 minutes cooking time.
5. Press the MATCH COOK button to copy the settings for Zone 2.
6. Initiate cooking by pressing the START/PAUSE BUTTON.
7. Garnish with lemon slices and herbs.
8. Serve warm.

Nutritional Information per Serving:

- Calories 401
- Total Fat 2.2 g
- Saturated Fat 2.4 g
- Cholesterol 110 mg
- Sodium 276 mg
- Total Carbs 25 g
- Fiber 1.4 g
- Sugar 1.4 g
- Protein 18.8 g

Shrimp Scampi

Prep Time: 10 minutes
Cooking Time: 13 minutes
Serving: 6

Ingredients

- 4 tbsp melted butter
- 1 tbsp lemon juice
- 1 tbsp minced garlic
- 2 tsp red pepper flakes
- 1 tbsp chopped chive
- 1 tbsp minced basil leaves
- 1 lb defrosted shrimp

Method:

1. Toss shrimp with melted butter, lemon juice, garlic, red pepper, chives and basil in a bowl.
2. Divide the shrimp in the two Air fryer baskets.
3. Return the Air Fryer Baskets to the Air Fryer.
4. Select the Air Fryer mode for Zone 1 with 390 degrees F temperature and 13 minutes cooking time.
5. Press the MATCH COOK button to copy the settings for Zone 2.
6. Initiate cooking by pressing the START/PAUSE BUTTON.
7. Toss the shrimp once cooked halfway through, and resume cooking.
8. Serve warm.

Nutritional Information per Serving:

- Calories 319
- Total Fat 19.7 g
- Saturated Fat 18.6 g
- Cholesterol 141 mg
- Sodium 193 mg
- Total Carbs 23.7 g
- Fiber 0.9 g
- Sugar 19.3 g
- Protein 25.2 g

Salmon Nuggets

Prep Time: 10 minutes
Cooking Time: 10 minutes
Serving: 2

Ingredients

- ⅓ cup maple syrup
- ¼ teaspoon ground dried chipotle pepper
- 1 pinch sea salt
- 1 ½ cups croutons
- 1 large egg
- 1 (1 pound) skinless, center-cut salmon fillet, cut into 1 1/2-inch chunks
- cooking spray

Method:

1. Mix chipotle powder, maple syrup, and salt in saucepan and cook on a simmer for 5 minutes.
2. Crush the croutons in a food processor and transfer to a bowl.
3. Beat egg in another shallow bowl.
4. Season the salmon chunks with sea salt.
5. Dip the salmon in the egg then coat with breadcrumbs.
6. Divide the coated salmon chunks in the two Air fryer baskets.
7. Return the Air Fryer Baskets to the Air Fryer.
8. Select the Air Fryer mode for Zone 1 with 390 degrees F temperature and 10 minutes cooking time.
9. Press the MATCH COOK button to copy the settings for Zone 2.
10. Initiate cooking by pressing the START/PAUSE BUTTON.
11. Flip the chunks once cooked halfway through, then resume cooking.
12. Pour the maple syrup on top and serve warm.

Nutritional Information per Serving:

- Calories 317
- Total Fat 11.9 g
- Saturated Fat 1.7 g
- Cholesterol 78 mg
- Sodium 79 mg
- Total Carbs 14.8 g
- Fiber 1.1 g
- Sugar 8.3 g
- Protein 25 g

Chapter 8: Vegetables

Easy Air Fried Tofu

Prep Time: 10 minutes
Cooking Time: 14 minutes
Serving: 6

Ingredients

- ⅔ cup coconut aminos
- 2 (14 oz) packages extra-firm, water-packed tofu, drained
- 6 tbsp toasted sesame oil
- ⅔ cup lime juice

Method:

1. Pat dry the tofu bars and slice into half-inch cubes.
2. Toss all the remaining ingredients in a small bowl.
3. Marinate for 4 hours in the refrigerator. Drain off the excess water.
4. Divide the tofu cubes in the two Air Fryer baskets.
5. Return the Air Fryer Baskets to the Air Fryer.
6. Select the Air Fryer mode for Zone 1 with 400 degrees F temperature and 14 minutes cooking time.
7. Press the MATCH COOK button to copy the settings for Zone 2.
8. Initiate cooking by pressing the START/PAUSE BUTTON.
9. Toss the tofu once cooked halfway through, then resume cooking.
10. Serve warm.

Nutritional Information per Serving:

- Calories 295
- Total Fat 3 g
- Saturated Fat 1 g
- Cholesterol 283 mg
- Sodium 355 mg
- Total Carbs 10 g
- Fiber 1 g
- Sugar 5 g
- Protein 1g

Chickpea Falafel

Prep Time: 10 minutes
Cooking Time: 14 minutes
Serving: 4

Ingredients

- 1 (15.5 oz) can chickpeas, rinsed and drained
- 1 small yellow onion, cut in quarters
- 3 garlic cloves, chopped
- 1/3 cup chopped parsley
- 1/3 cup chopped cilantro
- 1/3 cup chopped scallions
- 1 tsp cumin
- 1/2 tsp kosher salt
- 1/8 tsp crushed red pepper flakes
- 1 tsp baking powder
- 4 tbsp all-purpose flour
- Olive oil spray

Method:

1. Dry the chickpeas on paper towels.
2. Add onions and garlic to a food processor and chop them finely.
3. Add the parsley, salt, cilantro, scallions, cumin, and red pepper flakes.
4. Press the pulse button for 60 seconds, then toss in chickpeas and blend for 3 times until it makes a chunky paste.
5. Stir in baking powder and flour and mix well.
6. Transfer the falafel mixture to a bowl and cover to refrigerate for 3 hours.
7. Make 12 balls out the falafel mixture.
8. Place 6 falafels in each of the Air Fryer baskets and spray them with oil.
9. Return the Air Fryer Baskets to the Air Fryer.
10. Select the Air Fryer mode for Zone 1 with 350 degrees F temperature and 14 minutes cooking time.
11. Press the MATCH COOK button to copy the settings for Zone 2.
12. Initiate cooking by pressing the START/PAUSE BUTTON.
13. Toss the falafel once cooked halfway through, and resume cooking.
14. Serve warm

Nutritional Information per Serving:

- Calories 253
- Total Fat 8.9 g
- Saturated Fat 4.5 g
- Cholesterol 57 mg

- Sodium 340 mg
- Total Carbs 24.7 g
- Fiber 1.2 g
- Sugar 11.3 g
- Protein 5.3 g

Gingered Carrots

Prep Time: 10 minutes
Cooking Time: 25 minutes
Serving: 2

Ingredients

- 1 lb. cup carrots, cut into chunks
- 1 tbsp sesame oil
- ½ tbsp minced ginger
- ½ tbsp soy sauce
- ½ tsp minced garlic
- ½ tbsp chopped scallions, for garnish
- ½ tsp sesame seeds for garnish

Method:

1. Toss all the ginger carrots ingredients, except the sesame seeds and scallions, in a suitable bowl.
2. Divide the carrots in the two Air Fryer Baskets in a single layer.
3. Return the Air Fryer Baskets to the Air Fryer.
4. Select the Air Fryer mode for Zone 1 with 390 degrees F temperature and 25 minutes cooking time.
5. Press the MATCH COOK button to copy the settings for Zone 2.
6. Initiate cooking by pressing the START/PAUSE BUTTON.
7. Toss the carrots once cooked halfway through.
8. Garnish with sesame seeds and scallions.
9. Serve warm.

Nutritional Information per Serving:

- Calories 327
- Total Fat 31.1 g
- Saturated Fat 4.2 g
- Cholesterol 123 mg
- Sodium 86 mg
- Total Carbs 49 g
- Sugar 12.4 g
- Fiber 1.8 g
- Protein 13.5 g

Zucchini Fritters

Prep Time: 10 minutes
Cooking Time: 17 minutes
Serving: 4

Ingredients

- 2 medium zucchinis, grated
- 1 cup corn kernel
- 1 medium potato cooked
- 2 tbsp chickpea flour
- 2 garlic finely minced
- 2 tsp olive oil
- Salt and black pepper
- For Serving:
- Yogurt tahini sauce

Method:

1. Mix grated zucchini with a pinch of salt in a colander and leave them for 15 minutes.
2. Squeeze out their excess water.
3. Mash the cooked potato in a large-sized bowl with a fork.
4. Add zucchini, corn, garlic, chickpea flour, salt, and black pepper to the bowl.
5. Mix these fritters ingredients together and make 2 tbsp-sized balls out of this mixture and flatten them lightly.
6. Divide the fritters in the two Air Fryer baskets in a single layer and spray them with cooking.
7. Return the Air Fryer Baskets to the Air Fryer.
8. Select the Air Fryer mode for Zone 1 with 390 degrees F temperature and 17 minutes cooking time.
9. Press the MATCH COOK button to copy the settings for Zone 2.
10. Initiate cooking by pressing the START/PAUSE BUTTON.
11. Flip the fritters once cooked halfway through, then resume cooking.
12. Serve.

Nutritional Information per Serving:

- Calories 398
- Total Fat 13.8 g
- Saturated Fat 5.1 g
- Cholesterol 200 mg
- Sodium 272 mg
- Total Carbs 33.6 g
- Fiber 1 g
- Sugar 9.3 g
- Protein 1.8 g

Quinoa Burger

Prep Time: 10 minutes
Cooking Time: 13 minutes
Serving: 4

Ingredients

- 1 cup quinoa red, white or multi-colored
- 1½ cups water
- 1 tsp salt
- black pepper, ground
- 1½ cups rolled oats
- 3 eggs beaten
- ¼ cup minced white onion
- ½ cup crumbled feta cheese
- ¼ cup chopped fresh chives
- Salt and ground black pepper, to taste
- Vegetable or canola oil
- 4 hamburger buns
- 4 arugula
- 4 slices tomato sliced
- Cucumber yogurt dill sauce
- 1 cup cucumber, diced
- 1 cup Greek yogurt
- 2 tsp lemon juice
- ¼ tsp salt
- Black pepper, ground
- 1 tbsp chopped fresh dill
- 1 tbsp olive oil

Method:

1. Add quinoa to a saucepan filled with cold water, salt and black pepper and place it over medium high heat.
2. Cook the quinoa to a boil then reduce the heat, cover and cook for 20 minutes on a simmer.
3. Fluff and mix the cooked quinoa with a fork and remove it from the heat.
4. Spread the quinoa in a baking stay.
5. Mix eggs, oats, onion, herbs, cheese, salt and black pepper.
6. Stir in quinoa then mix well. Make 4 patties out of this quinoa cheese mixture.
7. Divide the patties in the two Air Fryer Baskets and spray them with cooking oil.
8. Return the Air Fryer Baskets to the Air Fryer.
9. Select the Air Fryer mode for Zone 1 with 390 degrees F temperature and 13 minutes cooking time.
10. Press the MATCH COOK button to copy the settings for Zone 2.
11. Initiate cooking by pressing the START/PAUSE BUTTON.
12. Flip the patties once cooked halfway through, and resume cooking.

13. Meanwhile, prepare the cucumber yogurt dill sauce by mixing all of its ingredients in a mixing bowl.
14. Place each quinoa patty in a burger bun along with arugula leaves.
15. Serve with yogurt dill sauce.

Nutritional Information per Serving:

- Calories 361
- Total Fat 15 g
- Saturated Fat 7 g
- Cholesterol 46 mg
- Sodium 108 mg
- Total Carbs 33 g
- Fiber 1 g
- Sugar 26 g
- Protein 4 g

Air Fried Okra

Prep Time: 10 minutes
Cooking Time: 13 minutes
Serving: 2

Ingredients

- ½ lb okra pods sliced
- 1 tsp olive oil
- ¼ tsp salt
- ⅛ tsp ground black pepper

Method:

1. Preheat your Air Fryer Machine to 350 F.
2. Toss okra with olive oil, salt, and black pepper in a bowl.
3. Spread the okra in a single layer in the two Air Fryer Baskets.
4. Return the Air Fryer Baskets to the Air Fryer.
5. Select the Air Fryer mode for Zone 1 with 375 degrees F temperature and 13 minutes cooking time.
6. Press the MATCH COOK button to copy the settings for Zone 2.
7. Initiate cooking by pressing the START/PAUSE BUTTON.
8. Toss the okra once cooked halfway through, and resume cooking.
9. Serve warm.

Nutritional Information per Serving:

- Calories 188
- Total Fat 1 g
- Saturated Fat 7 g
- Cholesterol 136 mg
- Sodium 128 mg
- Total Carbs 15 g
- Fiber 1 g
- Sugar 26 g
- Protein 4 g

Hasselback Potatoes

Prep Time: 10 minutes
Cooking Time: 25 minutes
Serving: 4

Ingredients

- 4 medium Yukon Gold potatoes
- 3 tbsp melted butter
- 1 tbsp olive oil
- 3 cloves garlic, crushed
- ½ tsp ground paprika
- Salt and black pepper ground, to taste
- 1 tbsp chopped fresh parsley

Method:

1. Slice each potato from top to make 1/4-inch slices, without cutting its 1/2-inch bottom, keeping the potato's bottom intact.
2. Mix butter, with olive oil, garlic, and paprika in a small bowl.
3. Brush the garlic mixture on top of each potato and add the mixture into the slits.
4. Season them with salt and black pepper.
5. Place 2 seasoned potatoes in each of the Air Fryer Baskets
6. Return the Air Fryer Baskets to the Air Fryer.
7. Select the Air Fryer mode for Zone 1 with 375 degrees F temperature and 25 minutes cooking time.
8. Press the MATCH COOK button to copy the settings for Zone 2.
9. Initiate cooking by pressing the START/PAUSE BUTTON.
10. Brushing the potatoes again with butter mixture after 15 minutes then resume cooking.
11. Garnish with parsley.
12. Serve warm.

Nutritional Information per Serving:

- Calories 362
- Total Fat 10 g
- Saturated Fat 9 g
- Cholesterol 326 mg
- Sodium 18 mg
- Total Carbs 48 g
- Fiber 1 g
- Sugar 2 g
- Protein 5 g

Chapter 9: Desserts

Mini Apple Pies

Prep Time: 10 minutes
Cooking Time: 25 minutes
Serving: 6

Ingredients

- 8 tbsp butter, softened
- 12 tbsp brown sugar
- 2 tsp cinnamon, ground
- 4 medium Granny Smith apples, diced
- 2 tsp cornstarch
- 4 tsp cold water
- 1 (14 oz) package pastry, 9-inch crust pie
- Cooking spray
- 1 tbsp grapeseed oil
- ½ cup powdered sugar
- 2 tsp milk

Method:

1. Toss apples, with brown sugar, butter, and cinnamon in a suitable skillet.
2. Place the skillet over medium heat and stir cook for 5 minutes.
3. Mix cornstarch with cold water in a small bowl.
4. Add cornstarch mixture into the apple and cook for 1 minute until it thickens.
5. Remove this filling from the heat and allow it to cool.
6. Unroll the pie crust and spray on a floured surface.
7. Cut the dough into 16 equal rectangles.
8. Wet the edges of the 8 rectangles with water and divide the apple filling at the center of these rectangles.
9. Place the other 8 rectangles on top and crimp the edges with a fork.
10. Place 4 small pies in each of the Air Fryer Baskets.
11. Return the Air Fryer Baskets to the Air Fryer.
12. Select the Air Fryer mode for Zone 1 with 390 degrees F temperature and 17 minutes cooking time.
13. Press the MATCH COOK button to copy the settings for Zone 2.
14. Initiate cooking by pressing the START/PAUSE BUTTON.
15. Flip the pies once cooked halfway through, and resume cooking.
16. Meanwhile, mix sugar with milk.

17. Pour this mixture over the apple pies.
18. Serve fresh.

Nutritional Information per Serving:

- Calories 271
- Total Fat 15 g
- Saturated Fat 7 g
- Cholesterol 46 mg
- Sodium 178 mg
- Total Carbs 33 g
- Fiber 1 g
- Sugar 26 g
- Protein 4 g

Walnuts Fritters

Prep Time: 10 minutes
Cooking Time: 15 minutes
Serving: 8

Ingredients

- Cooking spray
- 1 cup all-purpose flour
- ½ cup walnuts, coarsely chopped
- ¼ cup white sugar
- ¼ cup milk
- 1 egg
- 1 ½ tsp baking powder
- 1 pinch salt
- 2 tbsp white sugar
- ½ tsp ground cinnamon

Glaze:

- ½ cup confectioners' sugar
- 1 tbsp milk
- ½ tsp caramel extract
- ¼ tsp ground cinnamon

Method:

1. Layer both Air Fryer Baskets with parchment paper.
2. Grease the parchment paper with cooking spray.
3. Whisk flour with milk, 1/4 cup sugar, egg, baking powder, and salt in a small bowl.
4. Separately mix 2 tbsp sugar with cinnamon in another bowl, toss in walnuts and mix well to coat.
5. Stir in flour mixture and mix until combined.
6. Drop the fritters mixture using a cookie scoop into the two Air Fryer Baskets.
7. Return the Air Fryer Baskets to the Air Fryer.
8. Select the Air Fryer mode for Zone 1 with 375 degrees F temperature and 15 minutes cooking time.
9. Press the MATCH COOK button to copy the settings for Zone 2.
10. Initiate cooking by pressing the START/PAUSE BUTTON.
11. Flip the fritters once cooked halfway through, then resume cooking.
12. Meanwhile, whisk milk, caramel extract, confectioners' sugar, and cinnamon in a bowl.
13. Transfer fritters to a wire rack and allow them to cool.
14. Drizzle with glaze over the fritters.

Nutritional Information per Serving:

- Calories 146
- Total Fat 5 g
- Saturated Fat 7 g
- Cholesterol 46 mg
- Sodium 145 mg
- Total Carbs 16 g
- Fiber 1 g
- Sugar 13 g
- Protein 6 g

Air Fried Bananas

Prep Time: 10 minutes
Cooking Time: 13 minutes
Serving: 4

Ingredients

- 4 bananas, sliced into 1/8-inch thick diagonals
- 1 serving avocado oil cooking spray

Method:

1. Spread the banana slices in the two air fryer baskets in a single layer.
2. Drizzle avocado oil over the banana slices.
3. Return the Air Fryer Baskets to the Air Fryer.
4. Select the Air Fryer mode for Zone 1 with 350 degrees F temperature and 13 minutes cooking time.
5. Press the MATCH COOK button to copy the settings for Zone 2.
6. Initiate cooking by pressing the START/PAUSE BUTTON.
7. Serve.

Nutritional Information per Serving:

- Calories 171
- Total Fat 1 g
- Saturated Fat 2 g
- Cholesterol 6 mg
- Sodium 108 mg
- Total Carbs 23 g
- Fiber 1 g
- Sugar 6 g
- Protein 2 g

Crispy Beignets

Prep Time: 10 minutes
Cooking Time: 17 minutes
Serving: 6

Ingredients

- Cooking spray
- ¼ cup white sugar
- ⅛ cup water
- ½ cup all-purpose flour
- 1 large egg, separated
- 1 ½ tsp butter, melted
- ½ tsp baking powder
- ½ tsp vanilla extract
- 1 pinch salt
- 2 tbsp confectioners' sugar, or to taste

Method:

1. Beat flour with water, sugar, egg yolk, baking powder, butter, vanilla extract, and salt in a large bowl, until lumps-free.
2. Beat egg whites in a separate bowl and beat using an electric hand mixer until it forms soft peaks.
3. Add the egg white to the flour batter and mix gently until fully incorporated.
4. Divide the dough into small beignets and place them in the air fryer baskets.
5. Return the Air Fryer Baskets to the Air Fryer.
6. Select the Air Fryer mode for Zone 1 with 390 degrees F temperature and 17 minutes cooking time.
7. Press the MATCH COOK button to copy the settings for Zone 2.
8. Initiate cooking by pressing the START/PAUSE BUTTON.
9. And cook for another 4 minutes. Dust the cooked beignets with sugar.
10. Serve.

Nutritional Information per Serving:

- Calories 212
- Total Fat 8 g
- Saturated Fat 9 g
- Cholesterol 26 mg
- Sodium 153 mg
- Total Carbs 51 g
- Fiber 1 g
- Sugar 27 g
- Protein 3 g

Cinnamon Doughnuts

Prep Time: 10 minutes
Cooking Time: 15 minutes
Serving: 6

Ingredients

- 1 can pre-made biscuit dough
- ½ cup white sugar
- 1 tsp cinnamon
- ½ cup powdered sugar
- Coconut oil
- Melted butter, to brush biscuits

Method:

1. Place all the biscuits on a cutting board and cut holes in the center of each biscuit using a cookie cutter.
2. Grease the Air Fryer Baskets with coconut oil.
3. Place the biscuits in the two Air Fryers Baskets while keep them 1 inch apart.
4. Return the Air Fryer Baskets to the Air Fryer.
5. Select the Air Fryer mode for Zone 1 with 375 degrees F temperature and 15 minutes cooking time.
6. Press the MATCH COOK button to copy the settings for Zone 2.
7. Initiate cooking by pressing the START/PAUSE BUTTON.
8. Brush all the donuts with melted butter and sprinkle cinnamon and sugar on top.
9. Air fry these donuts for one minute more.
10. Enjoy.

Nutritional Information per Serving:

- Calories 282
- Total Fat 5 g
- Saturated Fat 12 g
- Cholesterol 116 mg
- Sodium 10 mg
- Total Carbs 25 g
- Fiber 1 g
- Sugar 26 g
- Protein 2 g

Cranberry Scones

Prep Time: 10 minutes
Cooking Time: 16 minutes
Serving: 4

Ingredients

- 4 cups of flour
- 1/2 cup brown sugar
- 2 tbsp baking powder
- ½ tsp ground nutmeg
- ½ tsp salt
- ½ cup butter, chilled and diced
- 2 cups fresh cranberry
- 2/3 cup sugar
- 2 tbsp orange zest
- 1 ¼ cup half and half cream
- 2 eggs

Method:

1. Whisk flour with baking powder, salt, nutmeg, and both the sugars in a bowl.
2. Stir in egg and cream, mix well to form a smooth dough.
3. Fold in cranberries along with the orange zest.
4. Knead this dough well on a work surface.
5. Cut 3-inch circles out of the dough.
6. Divide the scones in the Air Fryer Baskets and spray them cooking oil.
7. Return the Air Fryer Baskets to the Air Fryer.
8. Select the Air Fryer mode for Zone 1 with 375 degrees F temperature and 16 minutes cooking time.
9. Press the MATCH COOK button to copy the settings for Zone 2.
10. Initiate cooking by pressing the START/PAUSE BUTTON.
11. Flip the scones once cooked halfway and resume cooking.
12. Enjoy.

Nutritional Information per Serving:

- Calories 292
- Total Fat 2 g
- Saturated Fat 7 g
- Cholesterol 46 mg
- Sodium 112 mg
- Total Carbs 41 g
- Fiber 1 g
- Sugar 26 g
- Protein 4 g

Apple Flautas

Prep Time: 10 minutes
Cooking Time: 8 minutes
Serving: 6

Ingredients

- ¼ cup light brown sugar
- 1/8 cup all-purpose flour
- ¼ tsp ground cinnamon
- Nutmeg, to taste
- 4 apples, peeled, cored & sliced
- ½ lemon, juice, and zest
- 6 (10-inch) flour tortillas
- Vegetable oil
- Caramel sauce
- Cinnamon sugar

Method:

1. Preheat your Air Fryer machine at 400 F.
2. Mix brown sugar with cinnamon, nutmeg, and flour in a large bowl.
3. Toss in apples in lemon juice. Mix well.
4. Place a tortilla at a time on a flat surface and add ½ cup of the apple mixture to the tortilla.
5. Roll the tortilla into a burrito and seal it tightly and hold it in place with a toothpick.
6. Repeat the same steps with remaining tortillas and apple mixture.
7. Place two apple burritos in each of the Air Fryer Baskets and spray them with cooking oil.
8. Return the Air Fryer Baskets to the Air Fryer.
9. Select the Air Fryer mode for Zone 1 with 400 degrees F temperature and 8 minutes cooking time.
10. Press the MATCH COOK button to copy the settings for Zone 2.
11. Initiate cooking by pressing the START/PAUSE BUTTON.
12. Flip the burritos once cooked halfway through, then resume cooking.
13. Garnish with caramel sauce and cinnamon sugar.
14. Enjoy.

Nutritional Information per Serving:

- Calories 236
- Total Fat 5 g
- Saturated Fat 3 g
- Cholesterol 154 mg

- Sodium 113 mg
- Total Carbs 43 g
- Fiber 1 g
- Sugar 26 g
- Protein 6 g

Apple Oats Crisp

Prep Time: 10 minutes
Cooking Time: 14 minutes
Serving: 6

Ingredients

- 3 cups apples, chopped
- 1 tbsp pure maple syrup
- 2 tsp lemon juice
- 3 tbsp all-purpose flour, divided
- 1/3 cup quick oats
- ¼ cup brown sugar
- 2 tbsp light butter, melted
- ½ tsp cinnamon

Method:

1. Toss the chopped apples with 1 tbsp all-purpose flour, cinnamon, maple syrup, and lemon juice in a suitable bowl.
2. Divide the apples in the two air fryer baskets with their crisper plates.
3. Whisk oats, brown sugar, and remaining all-purpose flour in a small bowl.
4. Stir in melted butter then divide this mixture over the apples.
5. Return the Air Fryer Baskets to the Air Fryer.
6. Select the Bake mode for Zone 1 with 375 degrees F temperature and 14 minutes cooking time.
7. Press the MATCH COOK button to copy the settings for Zone 2.
8. Initiate cooking by pressing the START/PAUSE BUTTON.
9. Enjoy fresh.

Nutritional Information per Serving:

- Calories 264
- Total Fat 14 g
- Saturated Fat 9 g
- Cholesterol 46 mg
- Sodium 117 mg
- Total Carbs 33 g
- Fiber 1 g
- Sugar 26 g
- Protein 4 g

Conclusion

Wasn't it super quick and easy to cook a meal in the new Ninja 2 Basket Air fryer? Well, Its Dual-zone technology is really commendable, and it makes cooking a fun experience for all. It's about time that you give these recipes a try and see how convenient it will get while cooking in this new Ninja Air fryer.

Printed in Great Britain
by Amazon